For two S,
with

Joyce Holt
I hope you will enjoy
my book

More Share with Love
Canadian Cooking

More Share with Love Canadian Cooking

Joyce Holt & Gail Embury

Library of Congress Control Number:		2015919205
ISBN:	Hardcover	978-1-5144-2762-0
	Softcover	978-1-5144-2761-3
	eBook	978-1-5144-2760-6

Print information available on the last page.

Rev. date: 12/21/2015

To order additional copies of this book, contact:
Xlibris
1-888-795-4274
www.Xlibris.com
Orders@Xlibris.com
726619

CONTENTS

APPETIZERS

SOUP

SALADS

CHICKEN BEEF & PORK

FISH

CASSEROLES

VEGETABLES

PASTA AND RICE

BREADS AND BUNS

COOKIES

CAKES

MUFFINS AND LOAVES

PASTRIES AND DESSERTS

PRESERVES

Appetizers

Salmon Appetizers

6 slices	Thinly sliced bread, buttered
6 slices	Smoked salmon
1	Cucumber, sliced quite thin
1½ tsp	Yellow fish eggs

- Remove crusts from bread
- Lay smoked salmon on bread
- Cut bread into 4 triangles
- Place slice of cucumber on top of the salmon
- Garnish with yellow fish eggs

Makes 24

Shrimp Dip

1-8oz pkg	Cream cheese, softened
3 Tbsp	Milk
2 Tbsp	Grated onion
½ tsp	Worcestershire sauce
1 cup	Cooked shrimp, finely chopped

- Combine cream cheese and milk in a bowl and beat with an electric mixer until smooth
- Add onion and Worcestershire sauce and beat until fluffy
- Stir in the shrimp
- Serve with cracker or chips

Makes about 3 cups

Potted Ham Sandwiches

1-6 oz can	Potted ham
1 cup	Cottage cheese
2 Tbsp	Gherkins minced
12 slices	Whole wheat bread
	Salt and pepper

- Combine ham, cottage cheese, gherkins, salt and pepper and mix well
- Spread the mixture over 6 of the bread slices, top with remaining slices
- Wrap sandwiches and refrigerate for one hour
- Remove crusts, cut into quarters and serve

Makes 24

Salami with Cheese

6 slices	Salami
4 oz (¼ cup)	Cream cheese
2 oz (1/8 cup)	Blue cheese
4 tsp	Yogurt, plain
1½ tsp	Brandy
2 oz (1/8 cup)	Butter, softened

- Cut salami slices in half, roll up to form cones
- Beat together the cheeses, yogurt, brandy, and butter to make a stiff cream
- Fill each cone with the cheese mixture
- Garnish with a slice of red pepper

Makes 12

Shrimp and Caviar

8 cooked	Jumbo shrimp
½ cup	Mayonnaise (light)
4 slices	Thinly sliced bread
1 Tbsp	Lemon juice
¼ cup	Mayonnaise (light)
1/3 cup	Fish eggs
1	Lemon, thinly sliced and cut into wedges

- Split shrimp along the inside curl so that they are in two pieces.
- Transfer to a bowl and add ½ cup mayonnaise
- Toss gently and chill
- Toast the bread until lightly brown
- Brush toast with lemon juice and spread with the ¼ cup mayonnaise
- Cut each slice into four pieces
- Place a shrimp half on top of each piece, cut side down
- Pull the ends to make a nice curve
- Places ¼ tsp of fish eggs in the curve
- Garnish with a lemon wedge

Makes 16

Cucumber Appetizers

1	Long English Cucumber, sliced ¼-inch thick
1¼ tsp	White vinegar
¾ tsp	Sugar
1/3 cup	Water
	Pumpernickel bread, thinly sliced
	Butter
	Capers
	Pimento

- Butter pumpernickel bread slices
- Place cucumbers in a bowl
- Add vinegar and sugar plus enough water to cover cucumbers
- Let stand for ½ hour
- Drain and dry well on paper towel
- Cut pumpernickel into rounds, lay cucumber circles on top
- Garnish with 2 capers and small pieces of pimento

Makes approx. 2 - 2½ dozen

Crab Cocktail

1 dozen	Black olives, finely chopped
1 dozen	Green, stuffed olives, finely chopped
½ cup	Pickled onions, finely chopped
1 can	Crab, drained and cut up into small pieces
¼ cup	Ketchup
2 tsp	Worcestershire sauce
½ cup	Barbecue sauce

- Mix all ingredients together
- If the cocktail is too dry add 2 more tablespoons of either ketchup or barbecue sauce
- Refrigerate for about one hour
- Serve on shredded lettuce over ice

Note: if serving in cocktail glasses, fill bottom of glass with ice, fill insert with shredded lettuce and spoon cocktail over lettuce.

Serves 4

Cucumber and Salmon

1	English cucumber, 9 or 10 inches long
4 oz	Sliced smoked salmon, lox
3 large	Pickled onions, sliced
	Garlic salt
	Capers for garnish

- Cut cucumber into 1/3 – inch slices then cut edges with scalloped cookie cutter
- Cut salmon into smaller circles than cucumbers
- Place salmon on cucumber slices
- Garnish with sliced onions and capers

Serves 6

Carrot Canapés

1 cup	Carrots, finely grated
½ cup	Sweet pickle, finely chopped
½ cup	Mayonnaise
4 slices	Whole wheat bread, crusts removed, toasted and buttered
2 small	Dill pickles, thinly sliced
	Cucumber for garnish

- Combine carrots, pickles and mayonnaise in a small bowl
- Stir well and chill
- Spread filling on buttered toast
- Cut into triangles
- Garnish with cucumber

Serves 8

Cheese Balls

6 oz	Roquefort cheese
4 oz	Cheddar cheese, shredded
8 oz	Cream cheese
1½ Tbsp	Butter
1/3 cup	Walnuts, chopped and toasted

- Combine cheeses in a small bowl, beat with electric mixer until smooth
- Cover and chill
- Melt the butter in a small pan
- Add chopped walnuts and cook until well toasted, cool
- Roll cheese mixture into 1-inch balls and roll in toasted walnuts

Makes 20 - 24 balls

Garlic Toasts

3/4 cup	Butter
2 cloves	Garlic, crushed
6	English muffins, halved and toasted
	Parmesan cheese
	Salt and white pepper to taste

- Combine garlic, butter, salt and pepper, mix well
- Spread toasted muffin halves with garlic butter mixture
- Top with parmesan cheese
- Broil 2 to 3 minutes or until cheese melts and turns light brown

Makes 8 servings

Celery Sticks with Blue Cheese

7 oz	Blue cheese
1¼ cup	Cream cheese
2	Green onions, finely chopped
Dash	Black pepper
10 – 12 stalks	Celery
	Milk, as required
	Finely chopped walnuts
	Black pepper for garnish

- Combine blue cheese, cream cheese, green onions and pepper in food processor, mix until smooth
- If too thick, add a little bit of milk until consistency is spreadable
- Remove tough strings from celery
- Fill celery with cheese mixture
- Garnish with chopped walnuts and black pepper
- Cut celery into 2-inch pieces

Makes approximately 45

Prune Canapés

4 slices	White bread with crusts removed, toasted
1 Tbsp	Olive oil
4 thin slices	Cooked ham
1/3 cup	Cream cheese
¼ cup	Dried prunes, finely chopped
¼ cup	Pine nuts, finely chopped
	Chives, finely chopped

- Brush warm toast with olive oil
- Place slice of ham on each piece of toast
- Combine prunes, pine nuts and cream cheese, mix well
- Spread mixture over the ham
- Garnish with finely chopped chives
- Cut each slice into 4 pieces

Makes 16 pieces

Liver Pâté

8 oz	Cream cheese
8 oz	Liverwurst sausage
1 Tbsp	Minced green onion – white part only
½ tsp	Lemon juice
1 tsp	Worcestershire sauce
	Salt and pepper to taste
	Cocktail crackers

- In small bowl, using electric mixer on low speed, beat together cream cheese, liver sausage, and onion
- Beat in lemon juice, Worcestershire sauce salt and pepper
- Cover and chill for 1 hour
- Serve on cocktail crackers

Makes about 2 cups

Melon Punch

4 cups	Watermelon or honeydew melon, seeded and cubed
3 Tbsp	Frozen lemonade concentrate
½ cup	Club soda or 7-Up

- In blender or food processor combine melon and lemonade concentrate
- Blend until smooth
- Add club soda just before serving

Serves 6

Soup

Cream of Mushroom Soup

1 pound	White mushrooms, peeled
1½ Tbsp	Olive oil
¼ cup	Butter
1 small	Onion, finely diced
3 Tbsp	Flour
2¼ cups	Vegetable stock
2 cups	Milk
3 Tbsp	Half and half
	Salt and white pepper to taste

- Peel the mushrooms, separate the caps from the stems
- Slice the caps and chop the stems
- Heat the oil and half the butter in a sauce pan
- Add the onion, mushroom stems and half of the sliced mushroom caps
- Fry for about 3 to 5 minutes, stirring constantly
- Cover the pan, lower heat and let rest about 7 minutes, stirring occasionally
- Stir in the flour and cook for 2 minutes
- Gradually add the stock and milk and cook to a smooth, thin sauce
- Bring to a boil and simmer covered about 15 minutes
- Cool soup, pour into a processor or blender and blend until smooth
- In the pan, melt remaining butter, add rest of mushrooms caps and fry over low heat 3 to 5 minutes until they are just tender
- Pour the soup into a clean saucepan and stir in the fried mushrooms
- Heat until the soup is hot
- Add the half and half and serve

Serves 4

Creamy Asparagus Soup

2 pounds	Fresh asparagus, cut into 2-inch pieces
¼ cup	Onion, chopped
2 cups	Chicken broth
1 Tbsp	Butter or margarine
2 Tbsp	Flour
1 cup	Half and half
1 tsp	Fresh thyme, chopped (or ¼ tsp dried)

- In medium saucepan, combine asparagus, onion and broth
- Bring to a boil
- Reduce heat, cover and simmer 15 minutes or until asparagus is tender
- Cool about 5 minutes
- Place half of the asparagus mixture in blender or food processor and blend until smooth
- Repeat with remaining asparagus mixture
- Melt butter in medium saucepan, stir in flour
- Add half and half and thyme
- Cook and stir until thickened and bubbly
- Stir in asparagus mixture
- Cook 1 – 2 minutes or until thoroughly heated

Serves 4

Cold Peach Strawberry Soup

1	Peach, sliced
1 cup	Strawberries, sliced
1 cup	Yogurt – peach or strawberry flavour
1 – 2 Tbsp	Sugar
2 Tbsp	Lemon juice
	Lemon slices
	Fresh mint sprigs

- In food processor combine all ingredients except lemon slices and mint
- Process until smooth
- Pour into medium bowl
- Cover and refrigerate 1 – 2 hours or until thoroughly chilled
- Spoon into soup bowls
- Garnish with lemon slices and mint

Serves 5

Easy Soup

2 cups	Cooked chicken, cubed
2 cups	Frozen mixed vegetables
½ cup	Celery, chopped
1/3 cup	Onion, chopped
1/8 tsp	Thyme
1	Bay leaf
5 cups	Chicken broth
1 cup	Small macaroni (alphabet or ziti)
	Salt and pepper

- In a 4-quart saucepan combine chicken, mixed vegetables, celery, onion, thyme, bay leaf and chicken broth.
- Bring to a boil
- Reduce heat and stir in macaroni
- Simmer 10 – 15 minutes or until vegetables and macaroni are tender
- Remove bay leaf
- Season to taste

Serves 8

Potato Broccoli Soup

1 pkg	Scalloped potatoes with a sauce
3 cups	Water
1 cup	Milk
2 cans	Chicken broth
1½ cups	Broccoli, cut up
1 cup	Cheddar cheese, shredded

- In a large pot, combine potato slices, contents of sauce mix, water, milk and chicken broth; mix well
- Bring mixture to full boil
- Reduce heat, cover and simmer 15 minutes stirring occasionally
- Add broccoli to potato mixture; simmer 7 to 9 minutes or until broccoli is crisp tender
- Gently stir in the cheese until melted and well combined

Serves 6

Rice and Shrimp Soup

½ cup	Uncooked rice, rinsed
14 oz	Chicken broth
2 cans	Cream of mushroom soup
2 cups	Half and half cream
1 cup	Swiss cheese, shredded
¼ cup	Green onions, sliced
12 oz	Frozen, cooked shrimp

- Combine rice and chicken broth in a large saucepan; bring to a boil
- Reduce heat, cover and simmer 15 to 20 minutes or until rice is tender
- Stir in mushroom soup
- Add half and half cream, cheese and green onions
- Simmer until cheese is melted, stirring often
- Add shrimp; heat gently until shrimp are thoroughly heated, stirring often
- Do not boil

Serves 6

Pumpkin Soup

1 small	Onion, chopped
2 stalks	Celery, chopped
2½ Tbsp	Butter
1 can	Chicken broth
2 soup cans	Water
½ cup	Mayonnaise
1 can (28 oz)	Pumpkin
	Salt and pepper to taste

- Melt butter in a saucepan
- Cook celery and onion until tender
- Add chicken broth plus 2 soup cans of water
- Simmer 10 minutes or until vegetables are tender
- Add remaining ingredients plus salt and pepper to taste

Serves 8

Cream of Chicken Soup

4 cups	Chicken stock
2 cups	Celery, chopped fine
1 small clove	Garlic, pressed
¾ cup	Half and half cream
	Salt and pepper to taste
2 cups	Cooked chicken, finely chopped
½ cup	Grated parmesan cheese

- Pour stock into a large saucepan and bring to a boil
- Add celery and garlic, simmer for 10 minutes or until tender
- Pour into a blender and process until pureed then return to saucepan
- Add the cream, salt and pepper, bring just to the boil
- Stir in the chicken and the cheese; heat stirring until cheese is melted and soup is well blended
- Serve

Note: a dash of whipping cream may be poured into the centre of each serving if desired

Serves 8

Hamburger Soup

2 Tbsp	Vegetable oil
1 cup	Onion, chopped
¼ cup	Celery, chopped
1 pound	Ground beef
½ tsp	Salt
½ tsp	Pepper
½ cup	Green pepper, chopped
¼ cup	Red wine
1 cup	Kidney beans, rinsed and drained
3¼ cup	V-8 Juice

- Heat oil in large saucepan over medium heat
- When oil is hot, add onion and celery; sauté for a couple of minutes
- Add the beef and brown
- Add salt, pepper, green pepper, wine, kidney beans and V-8 Juice
- Bring to a boil
- Reduce heat and simmer for 30 minutes

Serves 4

Parsnip and Carrot Soup

1 cup	Parsnips, peeled and sliced
1 cup	Carrots, peeled and sliced
3 cups	Vegetable stock
2 cups	Milk
	Salt and pepper to taste
1/8 tsp	Nutmeg
¼ cup	Chives, chopped
4 Tbsp	Half and half cream

- In a medium saucepan, cook the parsnips and carrots in the vegetable stock until tender (about 12 – 15 minutes)
- Place cooked vegetables and broth in food processor and puree until smooth
- Rinse out the pot then return the puree to the pot
- Add milk, salt, pepper and nutmeg
- Reheat just to simmering
- Stir in the chives and half and half cream

Serves 4

Basic Beef Stock

2½ pounds	Beef bones with meat
10 cups	Water
1 cup	Celery, chopped
2	Carrots, cut in large pieces
1 medium	Onion, sliced
6 whole	Cloves
¾ tsp	Garlic salt
2	Bay leaves
1½ tsp	Dried basil
1½ tsp	Dried parsley
1½ tsp	Salt

Preheat oven to 375°F

- Brown meat and bones in oven, then place in a large saucepan with water and remaining ingredients
- Cover and bring to a boil
- Reduce heat and simmer for 4 ½ hours or until the meat is very tender
- The meat can be removed and added to the soup later.
- Pour the broth through a sieve and strain.
- Refrigerate
- When cold, remove the fat. This stock can be used in any soup or casserole calling for beef stock

Serves 6

Turkey and Yam Soup

2 Tbsp	Butter
1 small	Onion, thinly sliced
4 medium	Yams, cut into cubes
6 cups	Chicken broth
½ cup	Asparagus, cut into ½ inch slices
2 tsp	Salt
¼ tsp	Black pepper
3 cups	Cooked turkey, cut into ½ inch cubes

- In a large pot, melt butter over low heat
- Add onion and cook until tender
- Add yams, broth and 1 tsp salt; bring to a boil
- Reduce heat and simmer until yams are cooked
- Transfer ½ the soup to a food processor and puree.
- Return soup to the pot and add the asparagus and remaining salt and pepper
- Simmer until asparagus is just tender – about 6 or 7 minutes
- Stir in turkey cubes and cook about 4 to 5 minutes

Serves 8

Salads

Tropical Fruit Salad

Dressing

½ cup	Plain yogurt
2 Tbsp	Orange marmalade
¼ tsp	Poppy seeds

Salad

1 small	Pineapple, peeled and sliced
1	Mango, peeled and sliced
1 medium	Banana, sliced
1	Kiwi, peeled and sliced
2 Tbsp	Toasted coconut

- Combine all dressing ingredients in a small bowl, mix well
- Arrange fruit on a serving platter
- Drizzle dressing over the fruit
- Sprinkle with toasted coconut

Serves 6

Note: to toast coconut, spread on cookie sheet and bake at 350°F for 7 to 8 minutes or until light golden brown, stirring occasionally

Creamy Fruit and Pasta Salad

Dressing

4-oz	Cream cheese
2 Tbsp	Lime juice
2 Tbsp	Honey

Salad

½ cup	Uncooked pasta shells
½ cup	Cantaloupe, cubed
¼ cup	Seedless green grapes, halved
1	Peach, peeled and sliced
½ cup	Whipping cream, whipped
¼ cup	Fresh raspberries

- Combine all dressing ingredients in food processor and process until smooth, set aside
- Cook pasta to desired doneness; drain, rinse with cold water
- In large bowl, combine cooked pasta, cantaloupe, grapes and peaches
- Pour dressing over fruit, toss gently
- Cover and refrigerate 1 hour to blend flavours
- Garnish with raspberries and whipped cream just before serving

Serves 8

Four Veggie Slaw

Slaw

2 cups	Green cabbage, shredded
1 cup	Red cabbage, shredded
½ cup	Carrot, shredded
½ cup	Zucchini or cucumber, shredded

Dressing

¼ cup	Mayonnaise
2 tsp	Sugar
2 tsp	Cider vinegar
¼ tsp	Salt
Dash	Pepper

- Combine all vegetables in a large bowl
- In small bowl combine dressing ingredients, blend well
- Pour dressing over vegetables, toss lightly
- Serve immediately or cover and refrigerate until serving time

Serves 6

Shrimp Salad

3 cups	Cooked pasta shells, drained and cooled
2	Green onions, chopped
1/3 cup	Red pepper, diced
1/3 cup	Celery, diced
2/3 cup	Black olives, sliced
1 cup	Cooked shrimp
1/3 cup	Mayonnaise
1½ Tbsp	White balsamic vinegar
	Salt and pepper to taste

- Combine pasta, chopped onions, red pepper, and celery
- Add olives and shrimp
- Mix mayonnaise with balsamic vinegar, salt and pepper
- Add to pasta mixture
- Toss and serve

Serves 4 to 6

Lettuce and Prune Salad

8	Romaine leaves, torn into small pieces
2	Green onions, chopped
1 stalk	Celery, sliced
1/3 cup	Red pepper, chopped
6	Dried prunes, each cut into 6 pieces
2½ Tbsp	Mayonnaise
½ tsp	Sugar
2 Tbsp	Half and half cream

- Place lettuce in bowl
- Add green onions, celery, red pepper and prunes
- Mix mayonnaise with sugar and cream
- Toss vegetable mixture with mayonnaise mixture

Serves 4

Crab and Rice Salad

1 cup	Canned crab meat, drained
3 cups	White rice, cooked and cooled
¼ cup	Celery, sliced
¼ cup	Green pimento olives, sliced
¼ cup	Green peppers, diced
¼ cup	Onion, finely diced
½ tsp	Salt
¼ tsp	White pepper
4 Tbsp	Mayonnaise

- In a large bowl, combine crab meat, rice, celery, olives, green peppers, and onion
- Cover and chill
- Just before serving, stir together salt, pepper and mayonnaise and add to crab meat mixture
- Toss and serve on a bed of crisp greens

Serves 6

Pasta Salad

2 cups	Medium pasta shells, cooked and rinsed in cold water
1 1/3 cups	Canned cooked ham, cubed
3/4 cup	Tomato, chopped
3/4 cup	Mushrooms, sliced
¼ cup	Green pepper, chopped
¼ cup	Red pepper, chopped
1/3 cup	Green onions, chopped
1 cup	Mayonnaise
2 Tbsp	Lemon juice
½ tsp	Sugar

- In bowl combine pasta, ham, tomato, mushrooms green and red peppers, and green onions
- In separate bowl, combine mayonnaise lemon juice and sugar, mix well
- Add mayonnaise mixture to pasta mixture
- Cover and chill at least 30 minutes

Serves 8

Ham and Orange Salad

2 cups	Canned ham, cubed
1 cup	Celery, sliced
1/3 cup	Green onions, chopped
½ cup	Pine nuts
¼ cup	Pecans, chopped
1 can	Mandarin oranges, drained
¼ tsp	Pepper
1/3 cup	Mayonnaise
2 Tbsp	Half and half cream
1 Tbsp	White vinegar

- Combine ham, celery, onion, pine nuts, pecans, and oranges in a bowl, cover and chill
- Just before serving, blend pepper, mayonnaise, half and half and vinegar
- Pour over ham mixture, toss until well coated
- Serve on crisp lettuce or crisp spinach

Serves 6

Black Bean Salad

1 can	Black beans, drained and rinsed
2	Green onions, chopped
½ cup	Red peppers, chopped
½ cup	Green peppers, chopped
1 can	Yellow niblet corn
1/3 cup	Oil (olive or canola)
2 Tbsp	Lemon juice
½ tsp	Garlic salt
1 tsp	Chili powder

- Combine all ingredients
- Let rest 30 minutes then serve

Serves 6

Spinach Salad with Scallops

2	Oranges, peeled and segmented
1 cup	Orange juice
3 Tbsp	Balsamic vinegar
2 Tbsp	Shallots, minced
¼ cup	Olive oil
1 cup	Small scallops (or large ones cut into thirds)
2 Tbsp	Butter, melted
¼ tsp	Paprika
8 cups	Spinach leaves
2 Tbsp	Sliced almonds, toasted
¼ cup	Butter, chilled and cut into pieces

- Cut oranges between membranes to release segments
- Dressing: Mix juice, balsamic vinegar and shallots in a bowl; whisk in the oil
- Set aside ½ cup of mixture
- Pour remaining mixture in a small saucepan and simmer until reduced to ¼ cup (about 5 minutes), set aside
- Toss scallops with melted butter and season with paprika, salt and pepper
- Fry scallops until cooked through, about 3 to 5 minutes
- Toss spinach with reserved ½ cup dressing
- Mound spinach on plates and garnish with orange segments and almonds
- Bring dressing in the small saucepan back to a simmer and remove from heat
- Stir in cooled butter gradually and whisk until butter is just melted
- Place scallops on top of the spinach
- Drizzle sauce over scallops

Serves 8

Carrot Salad

1¾ cups	Carrots, shredded
¼ cup	Vegetable oil
½ cup	Almonds, slivered
½ cup	Dried cranberries
2	Green onions, sliced
½ cup	Mayonnaise
2 Tbsp	Half and half cream
	Salt and pepper to taste

- Place shredded carrots into a salad bowl
- In a skillet, add the oil, when hot, add almonds and toast to a light brown; remove and place on paper towel to dry
- Add almonds, cranberries and sliced green onion to the carrots
- Mix the mayonnaise with the half and half cream then add to carrot mixture
- Salt and pepper to taste

Serves 4 to 6

Orange and Avocado Salad

Salad

1 medium	Sweet onion
3 large	Oranges, peeled
2 large	Avocados, peeled and cubed
½ cup	Sunflower seeds, toasted
½ cup	Walnuts, toasted

Dressing

1/3 cup	Vegetable oil
1 tsp	Sugar
1 Tbsp	Balsamic vinegar
2 tsp	Orange peel, grated
¼ cup	Frozen orange juice, undiluted
¼ cup	Sherry or orange liqueur

- Combine all dressing ingredients in small bowl, set aside
- Peel and thinly slice the onion, separate into rings
- Slice oranges and combine with onions
- Add the avocados
- Pour the dressing over onions, oranges, and avocado
- Toss and refrigerate for up to 24 hours
- Just before serving, add the toasted sunflower seeds and walnuts

Serves 6

Bean Salad

2 cups	Kidney beans, drained and rinsed
2 cups	Chick peas, drained and rinsed
2 cups	White beans, drained and rinsed
1 small	Onion, thinly sliced
1 cup	Celery, diced
½ cup	Green pepper, diced
½ cup	Red pepper, diced
1/3 cup	White sugar
1/3 cup	Vegetable oil
½ tsp	Salt
½ tsp	Pepper
1/3 cup	White vinegar

- Combine the kidney beans, white beans and the chick peas
- Add all the vegetables
- Mix sugar, vinegar, vegetable oil salt and pepper and pour over the beans and vegetables
- Toss and chill

Serves 6 to 8

Spinach and Berry Salad

1 pkg	Fresh spinach leaves, washed and dried
1 cup	Strawberries, cleaned and halved
1 cup	Raspberries, cleaned
2 small or 1 large	Orange
1/3 cup	Walnuts, toasted
1/3 cup	Olive oil
3 Tbsp	White Balsamic vinegar
	Salt and pepper to taste

- Tear the large spinach leaves and put in to a medium / large salad bowl
- Add the strawberries and raspberries
- Peel the oranges, removing the white pith, then slice thinly removing any seeds
- Chop the walnuts and add to the bowl
- Whisk together oil, balsamic vinegar, salt and pepper
- Pour over salad toss together

Serves 6 to 8

Caesar Salad

3 slices	White bread, buttered and cubed
1 large	Romaine lettuce
3	Anchovy fillets
2 cloves	Garlic
1 Tbsp	Dijon mustard
	Black pepper
	Juice of 1 lemon
1/3 cup	Olive oil
¼ cup	Parmesan cheese

- Bake buttered and cubed bread in 350°F oven until golden and firm, set aside
- Wash and rinse lettuce leaves in plenty of cold running water
- Discard any tough stems then tear into small pieces
- Dry lettuce in salad spinner or on a towel
- Peel and chop garlic cloves
- Drain anchovy fillets, put them in a large bowl and crush them with a fork
- Add garlic, mustard and pepper to the anchovies
- Pour in lemon juice and olive oil and stir with a whisk
- Add lettuce to the dressing and toss until the leaves are well coated
- Add ½ the croutons and ½ the cheese then toss again
- Sprinkle remaining croutons and cheese on top
- Serve immediately

Serves 6 to 8

Chicken Beef & Pork

Chicken Cacciatore

¼ cup	Butter
2	2-pound broiling chickens, cut up
1 cup	Onion, chopped fine
1 cup	Green or red pepper, chopped fine
3 cloves	Garlic, minced
1 - 28 oz can	Tomatoes
1 cup	Tomato sauce
1 cup	Red wine
1 tsp	Salt
¼ tsp	Black pepper
3	Bay leaves
½ tsp	Thyme, crushed
1 cup	Black olives

- Melt butter in large skillet that has a tight fitting lid
- Brown the chicken on all sides in the butter
- Add the onions, chopped pepper, garlic, tomatoes and tomato sauce, mix well
- Stir in wine, salt and pepper then add bay leaves and thyme
- Cover tightly and cook over low heat for 35 – 40 minutes
- Turn chicken pieces once during this time
- Serve over cooked spaghetti
- Garnish with black olives

Serves 6

Glazed Chicken

4 whole	Chicken breasts
½ cup	Flour
1/3 cup	Vegetable oil
1 tsp	Salt
¼ tsp	Black pepper
1 8-oz bottle	Russian salad dressing
1 envelope	Dry onion soup mix
¼ cup	Brown sugar
2 Tbsp	Corn starch
¾ cup	Cider vinegar
1 Tbsp	Soy sauce
¼ tsp	Ground ginger
1	Chicken bouillon cube
1 can	Sliced pineapple drained (reserve juice)
1 large	Green pepper, sliced

Preheat oven to 350 °F

- Wash chicken and pat dry then roll in flour
- Heat oil in pan, add chicken and brown on all sides
- Place chicken in baking dish and sprinkle with salt and pepper
- In separate bowl, combine Russian dressing and onion soup mix and spread mixture on chicken (thin with water if it is too thick)
- Bake uncovered for 30 minutes
- Make glaze:
  - In a saucepan combine brown sugar, corn starch, pineapple juice, vinegar, soy sauce, ginger and bouillon cube
  - Bring to a boil and boil for two minutes
- Place pineapple slices and green pepper on top of chicken
- Pour glaze over chicken and bake 20 – 30 minutes uncovered until chicken is tender

Serves 4 – 6

Chicken Marsala

¼ cup	Flour
¼ tsp	Salt
¼ tsp	Black pepper
4	Chicken breasts, boneless/skinless
2 Tbsp	Olive or vegetable oil
2 cloves	Garlic, finely chopped
¼ cup	Fresh parsley, chopped
1 cup	Sliced mushrooms
½ cup	Marsala wine or chicken broth
	Hot cooked pasta

- Combine flour, salt and pepper in shallow plate
- Flatten each chicken breast to ¼-inch thickness
- Coat chicken with flour mixture, shake off excess
- Heat oil in 10-inch skillet over medium heat
- Cook garlic and parsley 3 to 4 minutes, stirring frequently
- Add chicken to skillet
- Cook until browned turning once
- Add mushrooms and wine
- Cook for 8 to 10 minutes turning chicken once until chicken is cooked through
- Serve with pasta

Serves 4

Chicken with Broccoli and Garlic Sauce

2 tsp	Olive oil
3 cloves	Garlic, minced
1 pound	Boneless/skinless chicken, cut into 1-inch pieces
1 tsp	Dried thyme
½ tsp	Salt
¼ tsp	Black pepper
2 cups	Uncooked broccoli florets
1½ cup	Chicken broth
1½ tsp	Cornstarch
2 cups	Cooked rice

- Heat oil in large skillet over medium-high heat
- Add garlic and cook 1 minute
- Add chicken, thyme, salt and pepper to skillet
- Cook chicken until browned on all sides, stirring frequently
- Add broccoli to skillet, cover and cook for 2 minutes
- Add 1 cup of broth, cover and simmer about 5 minutes
- Dissolve cornstarch in remaining ½ cup of broth and add to skillet
- Simmer until mixture thickens, stirring constantly, about 1 minute
- Serve over rice

Serves 4

Jambalaya

4 pounds	Chicken, cut into equal pieces
	Salt and pepper to taste
4 Tbsp	Bacon fat
6 Tbsp	Flour
1 pound	Lean smoked ham, diced
2 large	Onions, sliced thin
2 medium	Green peppers, seeded and sliced
5 medium	Tomatoes, skinned and chopped
2 cloves	Garlic, crushed
½ tsp	Dried thyme
2 cups	Long grain rice
1 ½ cups	Cold water
3 dashes	Tabasco sauce
½ pound	Cooked shrimp
3	Green onions, finely chopped
3 Tbsp	Parsley, chopped

- Season chicken with salt and pepper
- Melt bacon fat in large, heavy bottom pan and brown chicken on all sides
- Remove chicken from pan and lower heat
- Add flour to pan and stir constantly until mixture is light golden brown
- Return chicken to pan and add diced ham, onions, green pepper, tomatoes, garlic, and thyme.
- Cook for 10 minutes, stirring often.
- Stir rice into the pan with 1½ cups cold water and the Tabasco sauce
- Bring to a boil, reduce heat and cook until rice is tender and water is absorbed
- Add shrimp and ¾ of the green onions and ¾ of the parsley
- Use remaining green onions and parsley as a garnish
- Serve hot

Serves 8 to 10

Stuffed Cornish Game Hens

2 Tbsp	Butter
½ cup	Green onion, chopped
½ cup	Parsley, chopped
1 cup	Carrots, grated
½ cup	Celery, chopped
1 cup	Rice
3 cups	Chicken broth
½ tsp	Salt
1/8 tsp	White pepper
½ cup	Apricot jam

Preheat oven to 375°F

- Melt butter in a saucepan; add onions, parsley, carrots and celery and cook until tender, stirring often
- Add rice and stir until well mixed
- Add chicken broth, salt and pepper and bring to a boil
- Cook covered for 20 minutes or until the rice is done.
- Rinse out the game hens well and stuff the rice mixture into the hens
- Bake at 375°F for one hour
- Brush the tops of the hens with apricot jam and bake an additional 15 minutes
- Brush the tops of the hens again with the jam and bake for another 15 minutes

Serves 6

Chicken with Red Cabbage

2 pounds	Chicken breast cut into serving size pieces
2½ Tbsp	Olive oil
¼ cup	White wine
4 cups	Red cabbage, thinly sliced
6 cloves	Garlic, peeled
	Salt and pepper
½ tsp	Dried rosemary

Preheat oven to 325°F

- Season chicken with salt and pepper
- In a heavy saucepan, heat the olive oil over high heat
- Add chicken and brown for 5 minutes, turning once
- Remove chicken and place in a casserole dish
- Pour excess fat from the saucepan over the chicken
- Add wine to saucepan and stir constantly to loosen brown bits from the bottom of the pan
- Add the cabbage and garlic, stirring for two or three minutes
- Season to taste with salt and pepper
- Spread cabbage mixture evenly over the chicken, top with rosemary
- Cover tightly with foil and bake at 325°F for one hour

Serves 4 - 6

Turkey Meatballs

1 pound	Ground turkey
2 Tbsp	Cracker crumbs
2 Tbsp	Onion, chopped
1	Egg
1 tsp	Dried mint
1 tsp	Dried parsley
½ tsp	Salt
¾ tsp	Lemon pepper seasoning salt

- Combine all the ingredients, mix well and form into 1-inch meat balls
- Place on a broiler pan and broil about 6 inches from the heat for 8 to 12 minutes or until nicely browned
- Turn them occasionally so they brown on all sides

Serves 4

Lemon Chicken

4	Chicken breasts with skin on

Lemon Sauce

¼ cup	Butter
2 tsp	Grated lemon peel
2 Tbsp	Lemon juice
½ tsp	Salt
¼ tsp	Paprika
1 Tbsp	Fresh ginger, grated
Dash	Tabasco sauce

- Melt butter in small sauce pan over low heat
- Stir in lemon peel, lemon juice, salt, paprika, ginger and Tabasco sauce, set aside
- Place chicken, skin side down, on a rack in a shallow pan
- Broil 8 inches from the heat for 15 to 20 minutes, brushing occasionally with the lemon sauce
- Drain fat from the pan and turn chicken skin side up
- Broil 15 to 20 minutes longer or until tender, brushing from time to time with the sauce

Serves 4

Chicken Chow Mein

2 Tbsp	Oil
2	Onions, thinly sliced
1½ pounds	Chicken breast, cut into ½ inch cubes
3 cups	Celery, chopped
1½ cups	Chicken broth
3 Tbsp	Soy sauce
1 Tbsp	Fresh ginger
½ tsp	Salt
½ tsp	Sugar
1 can	Bean sprouts, drained
½ cup each	Broccoli and sliced carrots
¼ cup each	Red and green peppers
1½ Tbsp	Corn starch
1 can	Sliced mushrooms
1 can	Chow mein noodles

- In large fry pan, sauté onion in hot oil, add chicken and brown slightly
- Add celery, broth, soy sauce, ginger, salt and sugar
- Cover and cook for one hour
- Add bean sprouts, carrots, broccoli and peppers
- Mix cornstarch with 2 Tbsp cold water, stir into chicken mixture and cook until thickened
- Add mushrooms, cook 10 minutes longer
- Serve over chow mein noodles that have been warmed in a slow oven

Serves 6

Chicken Casserole

½ pound	Macaroni
3 Tbsp	Butter
3 Tbsp	Flour
¾ cup	Chicken stock
1½ cup	Light cream
1 tsp	Salt
1 can	Chicken
1/3 cup	Sliced canned mushrooms
1 cup	Frozen peas
	Dried fried onions

Preheat oven to 375°F

- Boil pasta until done then drain, set aside
- Melt butter in saucepan, blend in flour, stir until smooth
- Gradually add chicken stock and cream cook stirring constantly until thickened
- Add salt, set aside
- In a buttered casserole, make layers starting with pasta, chicken, mushrooms, peas and sauce then repeat until all ingredients are included
- Spread dried fried onions on top
- Bake at 375°F for 20 to 30 minutes

Serves 6

Glazed Buffalo Wings

30	Chicken wings, tips removed
2	Eggs, well beaten
1 tsp	Garlic salt
¼ tsp	Black pepper
¼ to 1/3 cup	Oil for frying
2½ cups	Barbecue sauce
2 Tbsp	Cornstarch
2 Tbsp	Cold water

- Preheat oven to 350 °F
- Rinse chicken wings and dry thoroughly
- Combine eggs, garlic salt and pepper in small bowl
- Heat the oil in saucepan to 350 °F – 360 °F
- Dip wings in egg mixture and fry a few at a time in hot oil until golden brown
- Drain wings on paper towels then place in shallow baking dish
- Pour barbecue sauce over wings and bake in oven for 20 – 25 minutes
- Mix cornstarch with 2 Tbsp cold water and add to sauce around the wings
- Place back in oven and cook additional 10 minutes or until sauce thickens
- Serve hot

Serves 4

Orange-Glazed Steak with Peach Salsa

Steak:

¼ cup	Soy sauce
2 cloves	Garlic, crushed
1 tsp	Black pepper
2 pounds	Round steak, 1½ - 2 inches thick

Salsa:

1½ pounds	Fresh peaches, peeled, pitted, & chopped
1 Tbsp	Red onion, finely chopped
1 Tbsp	Fresh mint leaves, chopped
1 tsp	Jalapeno pepper, seeded, finely chopped
1/8 tsp	salt

Steak:

- Combine soy sauce, garlic and pepper in glass baking dish
- Trim fat from steak, add to soy sauce mixture, and let stand for 30 minutes turning once
- Cook steak on grill or in oven until desired doneness, baste with marinade
- Serve with peach salsa on the side

Salsa

- Combine all ingredients in small bowl, stirring gently to combine
- Cover and refrigerate for at least 1 hour to blend flavours
- May be refrigerated up to 2 days

Makes 2 to 3 cups

American Beef Pot Roast

4 – 5 pound	Beef pot roast, any cut
2 tsp	Salt
¼ tsp	Pepper
1 clove	Garlic, chopped
2 – 3 Tbsp	Oil
¾ cup	Water
1 can	Beef broth
4 Tbsp	Ketchup
1 Tbsp	Worcestershire sauce
3 small	Onions, diced
2 – 3 Tbsp	Brown sugar
½ tsp	Dry mustard
3 Tbsp	Lemon juice
2 Tbsp	Flour
½ cup	Water

- Rub roast with salt, pepper and garlic
- Brown in hot oil
- Add water, beef broth, ketchup, Worcestershire sauce, and onions
- Cover and cook over low heat for 1½ hours
- Combine brown sugar, mustard and lemon juice and pour over meat
- Cover and continue cooking for an hour or until meat is tender
- Skim and pour off fat from gravy, discard
- Combine water and flour, mix to a paste
- Add to remaining liquid in pan, stir to thicken gravy

Serves 4 to 6

Ham Skillet Supper

3 cups	Medium egg noodles, uncooked
2 cups	Canned ham, cubed
1 Tbsp	Minced onion
1½ cups	Milk
1 tsp	Worcestershire sauce
1 (15 oz) can	Creamed corn
1 cup	Cheddar cheese, cubed

- Combine all ingredients in large skillet except cheese
- Mix well
- Bring to a boil
- Cover and simmer 18 to 20 minutes or until noodles are tender, stir occasionally
- Stir in cheese, cook until melted
- Serve immediately

Serves 4

Beef Noodle Stir-Fry

1 Tbsp	Oil
1 pound	Beef steak, cut into thin strips
1 (3 oz) pkg	Beef flavour instant ramen noodle soup
2/3 cup	Water
1/3 cup	Stir fry sauce
1 pound	Vegetables (any combination of broccoli, cauliflower, peas, peppers, carrots, etc)

- Heat oil in large skillet over medium/high heat
- Add beef and cook 3 – 5 minutes or until browned well
- Reduce heat to medium
- Break noodles into pieces and add to skillet
- Add soup seasoning packet, water, and stir fry sauce to skillet
- Bring to a boil stirring frequently.
- Cover and simmer 3 – 4 minutes
- Stir in vegetables
- Cook 2 – 4 minutes until noodles and vegetables are desired doneness

Serves 4

Corned Beef and Cabbage

4 – 5 pound	Brisket of corned beef
6 to 8	Carrots, peeled
6	Parsnips, peeled
4 medium	Onions, peeled
5 medium	Potatoes
1 medium	Cabbage, cored and quartered
	Parsley

- Place corned beef in large Dutch oven, cover with cold water and simmer, covered for 3 hours
- Skim carefully to remove excess fat.
- Add carrots, parsnips and onions, cover and cook for 30 minutes
- Add potatoes and continue cooking until potatoes are tender
- About 15 minutes before serving, add the cabbage and simmer
- Place meat in centre of a big platter, surround with vegetables and garnish with parsley

Serves 4 to 5

Rotini with Zucchini and Ham

1½ cups	Rotini or fusilli pasta, uncooked
2 Tbsp	Olive oil
1 cup	Carrots, sliced
½ cup	Onion, chopped
2 cups	Zucchini, sliced
8 ounces	Canned ham, cut into thin strips
¼ tsp	Dill seed (optional)

- Cook pasta to desired doneness, drain and keep warm
- Meanwhile, heat oil in large skillet
- Add carrots and onion, cook and stir 2 – 3 minutes or until crisp-tender
- Add zucchini, cook 1 – 2 minutes or until crisp-tender
- Stir in ham and dill seed, cook 1 – 2 minutes or until thoroughly heated
- Add cooked pasta to ham mixture, toss gently to combine

Serves 4

Baked Pork Chops

6	Pork chops, about ½ inch thick
¼ cup	Flour
1 tsp	Salt
1/8 tsp	Pepper
2 – 3 Tbsp	Vegetable oil
1 can	Cream of mushroom soup
¾ cup	Water
½ tsp	Grated fresh ginger
¾ cup	Canned French onions
½ cup	Sour cream

Preheat oven to350°F

- Mix together the flour, salt and pepper in a flat bowl
- Trim the fat from the pork chops
- Heat the oil in a skillet
- Coat the chops with the flour mixture and brown in the hot oil
- Place in a baking dish large enough to hold the pork chops
- Combine the soup, water, and ginger; pour over the chops
- Sprinkle ½ the onions over the chops
- Cover and bake at 350°F for 50 to 60 minutes or until meat is tender
- Uncover, sprinkle with the remaining onions and continue to bake another 10 minutes
- Remove chops to a platter
- Add sour cream to baking dish and blend well, heat and serve with the chops

Serves 6

Ground Beef Stroganoff

1 pound	Ground beef
1 medium	Onion, chopped
4 Tbsp	Flour
1, 10-oz can	Sliced mushrooms
1¼ cup	Beef stock
½ tsp	Salt
½ tsp	Dijon mustard
	Dash of black pepper
1 cup	Water
½ cup	Sour cream
1 tsp	Dried parsley flakes

- Brown the beef in a large skillet
- Add the onion and cook until the onions are tender
- Drain any excess fat then stir in the flour
- Add the mushrooms, beef stock, salt, mustard, pepper and water
- Bring to a boil; cover, reduce heat and simmer 8 to 10 minutes, stirring occasionally
- Stir in sour cream and parsley flakes
- Just heat through, do not boil after sour cream is added
- Serve over cooked egg noodles

Serves 4

Stuffed Pork Tenderloin

1 large	Pork tenderloin
2 Tbsp	Butter
1 large cup	Bread crumbs or Panko crumbs
1 small	Onion, finely chopped
½ tsp	Parsley (fresh or dried)
	Salt and pepper to taste

Preheat oven to 350°F

- Cut the tenderloin lengthwise making sure not to cut completely through
- After opening, flatten as much as possible, removing any excess fat
- Combine butter, bread crumbs (or Panko), onions, parsley, salt and pepper
- Spread the crumb mixture in the centre of the flattened tenderloin then fold it together again
- Roll up and tie with string
- Place in oven proof pan and bake at 350°F for 45 to 60 minutes until meat thermometer reads 170°F

Serves 6

Wiener Schnitzel

6 large	Slices of Veal, (thinly sliced)
	Salt and pepper
1 cup	Flour (in a separate bowl)
2	Eggs, beaten well (in a separate bowl)
1½ cup	Bread crumbs (in a separate bowl)
¼ cup	Butter
¼ cup	Oil

- Sprinkle meat on both sides with salt and pepper then dip into the flour
- Shake off excess flour then dip into the beaten egg then into the crumbs
- Coat meat completely, pressing crumbs firmly so that they don't come off
- Let stand at room temperature for one hour to dry
- Heat butter and oil in a large skillet and brown veal on both sides until cooked thoroughly

Note: Schnitzels can also be made using 6 large slices of pork

Serves 6

Roast Beef

5 pounds	Roast of beef (inside round)
2/3 cup	Flour
2 Tbsp	Dry mustard
1 tsp	Salt
¼ tsp	Pepper

Preheat oven to 450°F

- Place flour, mustard, salt and pepper in a plastic bag; shake well to mix
- Wipe the roast dry then place in the bag with the flour mixture
- Close the bag and shake until the roast is well coated
- Cook in oven for 25 minutes at 450°F then lower the heat to 350°F
- Cook an additional 1 hour (for rare) 20 minutes longer for medium rare
- Remove roast from oven, cover and let rest 15 minutes before serving

Serves 6

Yorkshire Pudding

3	Eggs
1 cup	Flour
½ tsp	Salt
1 cup	milk

Preheat oven to 400°F

- In a blender put eggs first then flour, salt and milk
- Mix until well blended, let stand for at least 30 minutes
- Place muffin pans in oven to preheat, when hot remove from oven, carefully grease with oil
- Stir batter and pour into muffin pan (approx. 2/3 full), bake at 400°F for 25 – 30 minutes

Makes 12

Meat Loaf

2 medium	Eggs
2/3 cup	Milk
2 tsp	Salt
¼ tsp	Pepper
3 slices	Fresh bread, crumbled
1 medium	Onion, chopped
½ cup	Carrot, shredded
1 cup	Cheddar cheese, shredded
1½ pounds	Ground beef
¼ cup	Brown sugar
¼ cup	Ketchup
1 Tbsp	Dijon mustard

Preheat oven to 350°F

- Break eggs into a large mixing bowl, beat lightly with a fork
- Add milk, salt, pepper and crumbled bread
- Mix until bread is soft and smooth
- Add onion, carrot, cheese and ground beef, mixing really well
- Pack into a 9 x 5 loaf pan
- Combine brown sugar, ketchup and mustard; spread over the meat
- Bake at 350°F for one hour
- Let stand about 10 minutes before removing from the pan

Note: Leftovers are very good served cold

Makes 8 hot slices

Baked Corned Beef

2 cups	Macaroni, uncooked
1 can	Cream of mushroom soup
1 cup	Milk
½ cup	Cheddar cheese, cut into small cubes
1 can	Corned beef, chopped
2/3 cup	Onion, chopped
1 cup	Panko crumbs
4 Tbsp	Butter

Preheat oven to 375°F

- Cook macaroni in boiling, salted water until done; drain
- Combine the cheddar cheese, corned beef and onion, set aside
- Mix the mushroom soup and the milk together until smooth, set aside
- In a casserole dish, make layers of macaroni, corned beef mixture, and soup mixture
- Bake at 375°F for ½ hour.
- Mix Panko and butter together, sprinkle over casserole and return to oven for another ½ hour.

Serves 4

Baked Pork Chops

6	Pork chops
2 Tbsp	Butter
1-10 oz can	Cream of mushroom soup
1 stalk	Celery
2	Green onions, chopped
¼ tsp	Salt (or to taste)
1/8 tsp	Pepper
½ cup	Water
¼ cup	Slivered almonds

Preheat oven to 350°F

- Brown pork chops in butter and set aside
- In medium bowl, combine mushroom soup, celery, onions, salt, pepper and water and beat with a spoon until well blended
- Place pork chops in an oven proof pan
- Pour sauce over chops and bake at 350°F for 40 minutes
- Sprinkle slivered almonds on top of chops and bake another 15 minutes or until meat is done

Serves 6

Cold Meat

5 pounds	Extra lean hamburger
2½ tsp	Mustard seed
2½ tsp	Garlic salt
5 tsp	Salt
1 tsp	Pickling salt
2½ tsp	Coarse pepper
2 tsp	Chili peppers
2tsp	Oregano
1 tsp	Marjoram

- Mix all the ingredients together and refrigerate
- Knead well every day for 3 days
- On the 4th day, shape into 4 or 5 small rolls
- Set oven at 175°F
- Using a broiler pan, cook the rolls for 8 hours, turning after 4 hours
- Can be eaten cold or reheated

Can be sliced and used as an appetizer or in sandwiches

Fish

Baked Filet of Sole

2 pounds	Filet of sole
2 Tbsp	Butter OR oil
1 cup	Soft bread crumbs
½ cup	Parmesan cheese, grated
	Thyme, to taste
	Parsley, to taste, minced
	Salt and pepper to taste
1 – 2 Tbsp	Melted butter
	paprika

Preheat oven to 350°F

- Grease a baking sheet with the butter or oil
- Combine bread crumbs, grated cheese, thyme and parsley salt and pepper
- Sprinkle mixture over baking sheet then place fish on top
- Drizzle a little melted butter over the fish and bake at 350 °F for 15 to 20 minutes or until fish flakes easily
- Sprinkle with more minced parsley and paprika and serve immediately

Serves 6

Fried Salmon Steaks

4	Salmon steaks, about 1-inch thick
3	Oranges
3 Tbsp	Butter
	Salt and pepper to taste

- Pat each salmon steak dry with paper towel and set aside
- Slice one orange into even slices
- Juice the remaining oranges, set aside.
- Melt the butter in a frying pan
- Add the salmon steaks and cook for 3 minutes on each side
- Add the juice to the frying pan and place orange slices on each steak
- Cover and poach the salmon in the orange juice until the salmon is cooked; about 5 to 6 minutes.

Serves 4

Pan Fried Trout

6	Trout
12 slices	Bacon
1	Egg
¼ cup	Milk
1 tsp	Salt
1/8 tsp	White pepper
¾ cup	Flour
1 tsp	Dried parsley

- Rinse trout under cold water and pat dry
- Fry bacon until crisp, remove from pan reserving bacon fat
- Keep bacon warm in the oven
- In a bowl, beat the egg lightly, then add the milk, salt and pepper
- In another bowl, combine the flour and dried parsley
- Dip the fish first in the egg mixture then coat in the flour mixture
- Fry in the hot bacon fat (add some oil if more is needed) for 2 to 3 minutes on each side or until the fish are cooked (at the thickest point of the fish it is nearly opaque and flakes easily with a fork)
- Drain fish and garnish with the bacon

Serves 6

Sole with Almonds

12 oz	Sole
3 Tbsp	Flour
½ cup	Butter
2	Lemons, juiced
2 Tbsp	Extra butter
1/3 cup	Almonds, sliced or slivered
	Salt and pepper to taste
1½ Tbsp	Chives, chopped

- Pat fish dry with paper towels
- Put flour in plastic bag and season with salt and pepper
- Add the sole to the flour and shake carefully
- Melt ½ cup butter in frying pan and add ½ of the lemon juice
- When butter starts to foam, add the fish
- Cover, reduce heat to low and cook for 4 minutes on each side or until fish is opaque, flakes easily, and the outside is a nice brown
- Transfer fish to a warm serving dish and keep warm
- Wipe frying pan clean and melt the 2Tbsp butter
- Add remaining lemon juice, almonds salt and pepper
- Bring to a boil and pour over fish
- Serve immediately

Serves 4

Tuna Stuffed Peppers

6 medium	Green peppers
1 – 7 oz can	Tuna fish, drained
2 cups	Cooked rice
1/3 cup	Onion, chopped
7½ oz	Tomato sauce
1	Egg, well beaten
2 Tbsp	Lemon juice
1 tsp	Salt
1/8 tsp	Pepper
1/8 tsp	Rosemary
	Grated parmesan cheese

Preheat oven to 400 °F

- Remove the stem, seeds, and membranes from the green peppers
- Parboil peppers 7 to 8 minutes and drain
- Combine tuna, rice, onion, tomato sauce, egg, lemon juice, salt, pepper and rosemary; mix well to blend
- Spoon this mixture into the green peppers and sprinkle tops with parmesan cheese
- Place peppers in greased baking dish and bake at 400°F for 15 to 20 minutes

Serves 6

Broiled Salmon Steaks

½ cup	Brown sugar
1 Tbsp	Mustard powder
1 Tbsp	Allspice
4	Salmon steaks, 1-inch thick
1	Long English cucumber
5 or 6	Green onions
2 Tbsp	Butter
1 Tbsp	Lemon juice
1 tsp	Dry dill weed
1 tsp	Dry parsley
	Salt and pepper

Preheat broiler in oven

- Mix sugar, mustard and allspice together and rub into both sides of the salmon steaks
- Place salmon in fridge covered, and let stand for at least 1 hour
- Peel the cucumber, cut into quarters lengthwise then cut each quarter into 1-inch pieces
- Trim the roots from the green onions and cut down some of the green part (but not all of it)
- Put cucumber and green onions into a saucepan with the butter, lemon juice, dill, salt and pepper and parsley
- Cook over medium heat for about 8 minutes or until the cucumber is tender
- Put salmon steaks under preheated broiler and cook for about 4 to 5 minutes on each side
- Serve with the cucumber and onions

Serves 4

Sole Fillets in Court Bouillon

Court Bouillon:

2 medium	Carrots, peeled and chopped
1 medium	Onion, peeled and chopped
1	Bay leaf
¼ cup	Vinegar
4 cups	Cold water

- Place all ingredients in a 2-quart saucepan
- Bring to a boil, reduce heat and simmer for 25 minutes
- Cool to lukewarm then strain

Sole:

4	Sole fillets
¼ cup	Butter
2 tsp	Vinegar
1½ Tbsp	Capers
1½ Tbsp	Fresh parsley, chopped or ¾ tsp dried

- Pour court bouillon into a skillet (skillet should be large enough to hold the fish as well) and bring to a simmer
- Place the fillets into the court bouillon, cover and poach about 5 minutes or until fillets are tender
- Remove fillets to a heated plate
- Melt the butter in a pan over medium heat
- Shake the pan until the butter is a dark brown
- Add the vinegar when the bubbles stop
- Pour over the fillets
- Garnish with the capers and parsley

Serves 4

Clam Soufflé

1 – 5 oz can	Minced clams
3 slices	Bacon, diced
¼ cup	Butter
¼ cup	Flour
1 cup	Milk
½ tsp	Worcestershire sauce
1 tsp	Salt
¼ tsp	White pepper
¼ tsp	Rosemary
3	Eggs, separated

Preheat oven to 375°F

- Drain clams, reserving the liquid. Add water to liquid to make ½ cup
- Sauté diced bacon, drain and set aside
- In a saucepan over medium heat, melt the butter, add the flour and blend well.
- Gradually add milk stirring constantly until the sauce thickens.
- Add the clams, reserved liquid and bacon
- Continue to cook over medium heat stirring for 5 minutes
- Remove from heat, add Worcestershire sauce, salt, pepper and rosemary; cool slightly
- Beat egg yolks well, add to clam mixture and cook 5 minutes over medium heat stirring constantly
- Remove from heat and cool (about 5 minutes)
- Beat egg whites until stiff but not dry; and fold into the clam mixture
- Pour into a greased baking dish placed inside a pan of hot water and bake at 375°F for45 to 50 minutes or until a toothpick inserted in the centre comes out clean

Serves 3 or 4

Salmon Steaks

4   Salmon steaks ½" to ¾" thick

Marinade:

1/3 cup	Rye whiskey
2 Tbsp	Soy sauce
½ cup	Vegetable oil
1 Tbsp	Garlic powder
1 tsp	Salt
1/8 tsp	White pepper
1 Tbsp	Brown sugar

- Combine all marinade ingredients
- Pour over salmon and let sit for 2 hours in the fridge
- Cook on an oiled grill about 4 to 5 minutes per side brushing often with marinade
- Fish is done when it flakes easily

Serves 4

Baked Cod

1 pound	Codfish, coarsely chopped
2 Tbsp	Green pepper, minced
1 Tbsp	Green onion, minced
4	Eggs, well beaten
2 cups	Half and half cream
1 tsp	Salt
¼ tsp	White pepper
1/8 tsp	Nutmeg
¼ tsp	Grated lemon rind

Preheat oven to350°F

- Combine fish, green pepper and green onion
- Place fish in a well-greased casserole
- In a bowl, beat the eggs well then add the cream, salt, pepper, nutmeg, lemon rind
- Pour the egg mixture over the fish
- Bake at 350°F for 30 to 35 minutes or until fish flakes easily in the centre

Serves 4

Curried Shrimp

2 Tbsp	Butter
1 small	Onion, chopped
1 clove	Garlic, minced
4 Tbsp	Flour
2 cups	Milk
3 Tbsp	Curry powder
½ tsp	Salt
¼ tsp	Black pepper
1½ cups	Frozen peas
35	Cooked (frozen) shrimp

- Melt the butter in large pan, sauté the onion and garlic for 1½ to 2 minutes
- Add the flour and stir well
- Gradually add the milk
- When sauce starts to thicken and becomes smooth, add the curry powder, salt and pepper stirring until the sauce is smooth and thickened
- Add the frozen peas, cook for 3 minutes
- Add shrimp and heat through, 3 to 4 minutes
- Serve over cooked rice

Serves 4

Baked Salmon

2-7½ oz cans	Salmon
3 Tbsp	Lemon juice
¼ tsp	Salt
2 tsp	Vinegar
1 cup	Sour cream
3 slices	Onion, separated into rings

Preheat oven to 325°F

- Drain the juice from the salmon
- Remove the center bone and any pieces of skin
- Place salmon in a 1-quart casserole
- Pour lemon juice over the salmon sprinkle with salt
- Mix vinegar with sour cream and pour over the salmon
- Lay onion rings on top
- Bake at 325°F for 40 minutes or until salmon is hot and cream is reduced to a rich sauce

Serves 4

Casseroles

Beans and Rice

2 cups	Cooked rice
1 – 15 oz. can	Black beans, rinsed and drained
1 cup	Frozen corn or 1 can Niblet corn
1 – 10 oz. can	Diced tomatoes
1 cup	Salsa
1 cup	Sour cream
2 cups	Shredded Mexican cheese blend, divided
1 small	Red onion, chopped
1 small can	Sliced black olives

Preheat oven to 350 °F

- In large bowl, combine beans, corn, tomatoes, salsa, sour cream, 1 cup of the shredded cheese and cooked rice
- Season with salt and pepper and combine well
- Transfer to greased 2-quart baking dish
- Top with onions and olives
- Bake uncovered at 350 °F for 30 minutes
- Sprinkle with remaining cheese and bake 5 – 10 minutes longer, until cheese is melted

Serves 8

Squash Casserole

3 pounds	Hubbard squash
2 Tbsp	Butter
1 cup	Sour cream
½ cup	Onion, finely chopped
1 tsp	Salt
¼ tsp	Pepper
	Dried, fried onions

Preheat oven to 400°F

- Cut squash into pieces, remove seeds, fibers and rind
- Cut into cubes
- In a large pot, bring 1 inch of salted water to a boil
- Add the squash, cover, return to the boil and cook for 15 to 20 minutes or until tender; drain
- Mash the squash, stir in the butter, sour cream, onion, salt and pepper
- Turn mixture into an ungreased 1-quart casserole, top with dried fried onions
- Bake at 400°F uncovered 20 to 30 minutes

Serves 6 to 8

Broccoli Casserole

2½ cups	Broccoli
1¼ cup	Milk
3	Eggs, slightly beaten
½ tsp	Salt
½ tsp	Chives, finely chopped
½ cup	Grated cheddar cheese

Preheat oven to 350°F

- Cook the broccoli in a small amount of boiling water for 3 minutes, then drain
- Pour the milk into a small saucepan and bring to a boil; cool to lukewarm
- Mix the eggs with the salt and chives
- Add the milk and cheese beating constantly
- Pour mixture into a greased baking dish then add the broccoli
- Bake at 350°F 30 to 40 minutes or until a knife inserted in the centre comes out clean

Serves 4 or 5

Scalloped Potatoes

**Dairy and gluten free

2 cups	Rice or soy milk
8 Tbsp	Rice or potato flour
2 Tbsp	Oil
½ tsp	Salt
¼ tsp	White pepper
4 medium	Potatoes, peeled and sliced thinly
1 medium	Onion, peeled and sliced
¼ tsp	Paprika
	Chopped green onions or chives for garnish

Preheat oven to 375°F

- Place 1½ cups of the milk in a saucepan and heat to a boil, set aside
- Take remaining milk and mix with the flour to make a paste
- Add the oil to the paste and stir until thick and smooth
- Add the salt and white pepper
- Stir into the hot milk – do not boil
- Place the thinly sliced potatoes and onions in layers in a greased casserole
- Pour sauce over the vegetables, sprinkle with paprika
- Bake at 375°F for approximately 1 hour and 15 minutes or until the potatoes are done and the top is golden brown
- Remove from oven and let stand for 10 minutes
- Garnish with the chopped green onions or chives

Serves 8

Seafood Casserole

3 cups	Minute rice
2 tins	Crabmeat, drained (save ¼ cup for garnish)
4 tins	Shrimp, drained (save ¼ cup for garnish)
3 tins	Mushroom soup
1/3 cup	Onion, grated
1 cup	Celery, chopped
1 cup	Green pepper, chopped
1-4 oz tin	Pimento, drained and chopped
2 Tbsp	Lemon juice

Preheat oven to 350°F

- Cook rice
- Add all the other ingredients to the rice
- Place into a 4-quart casserole dish
- Bake at 350°F for one hour uncovered
- Garnish with the saved crabmeat and shrimp

Serves 10 to 12

Tuna Crepe Casserole

Pancake

2	Egg yolks
½ tsp	Salt
1 cup	Light cream
½ cup	Flour
	Butter

- Beat egg yolks with salt and cream, beat in the flour
- Lightly butter a heated 7-inch fry pan and add 2 Tbsp batter
- Tilt the pan to cover bottom of pan evenly, then lightly brown each side
- Repeat until all batter is used; cover while making the filling

Preheat oven to 400°F

Filling

¼ pound	Mushrooms, sliced
2 Tbsp	Butter
2 Tbsp	Flour
1½ cups	Milk
2 cans	Tuna fish, drained well
1 Tbsp	Parsley, chopped
½ cup	Swiss cheese, grated
½ tsp	Salt
Dash	Black pepper, fresh ground

- In a saucepan, sauté mushrooms in butter (about 3 minutes)
- Add flour, salt and pepper then gradually add milk and cook, stirring constantly
- Boil for one minute then add tuna and parsley
- Spoon filling into centre of each crepe, roll up and place rolls in a 8 x 12 shallow casserole
- Dot with butter, sprinkle with the cheese and bake at 400°F 10 to 15 minutes

Serves 4 to 6

Fresh Corn Casserole

8 ears	Fresh corn
2	Eggs, well beaten
2 Tbsp	Onion, grated
¼ cup	Butter, melted
¼ tsp	Salt
Dash	White pepper
¾ cup	Milk

Preheat oven to 350°F

- Remove husks from corn
- Remove all the corn from the cobs
- In a mixing bowl, combine eggs and onion and mix well
- Stir in the butter, salt, pepper and milk
- Add the corn and mix together
- Place in a buttered baking dish and bake at 350°F for 40 minutes or until set in the centre

Serves 4 to 6

Stuffed Zucchini

6	Zucchini, each about 6 inches long
½ pound	Fresh mushrooms, chopped
¼ cup	Onion, chopped
¼ cup	Butter
1 Tbsp	Parsley, chopped
	Salt and pepper to taste

Preheat oven to 325°F

- Wash and dry zucchini and remove the stem and blossom ends
- Cut zucchini in half, lengthwise
- Create shells by scooping the flesh out the centre of each zucchini
- Chop the zucchini flesh fine
- Add the mushrooms and onion to the chopped zucchini and sauté in butter for about 5 minutes
- Stir in the parsley and season with salt and pepper to taste
- Stuff this mixture into the zucchini shells then put the zucchini halves back together again (one on top of the other)
- Bake at 325°F until tender, about 30 minutes

Serves 6

Cabbage Casserole

1 medium	Cabbage, shredded
1 pound	Ground beef
1	Onion chopped
½ cup	Rice, uncooked
	Salt and pepper to taste
1 can	Tomato soup
1 soup can of	Water

Preheat oven to 350°F

- Place cabbage in a greased baking dish
- Brown beef and onion in skillet
- Stir in the rice
- Place mixture on the cabbage, season with salt and pepper
- Combine soup and water and pour over the cabbage
- Cover with foil and bake at 350°F for one hour

Serves 6

Corn and Rice Casserole

¼ cup	Butter
1/3 cup	Onion, chopped
½ cup	Celery, chopped
1 can	Cream corn
1 cup	Long grained rice
¼ Tsp	White pepper
1½ cup	Water
	Parsley, finely chopped

Preheat oven to 350°F

- Melt butter in medium fry pan
- Add onions and celery and fry for 3 to 4 minutes
- Add the creamed corn and cook another 3 to 4 minutes
- Add the rice, white pepper and water
- Transfer mixture to a casserole and bake at 350°F for one hour
- Garnish with finely chopped parsley

Serves 6 to 8

Vegetables

Peas and Onions

2 pounds	Fresh peas, shelled
½ pound	Small pickling onions
½ cup	Vegetable stock
8	Romaine lettuce leaves torn into small pieces
3 Tbsp	Sour cream
1 tsp	Sugar
Dash	White pepper
	Salt to taste
2 tsp	Fresh mint, chopped

- Place peas and onions in boiling, salted water for 2 minutes, then drain and return to pot
- Add the vegetable stock, lettuce, and sour cream and bring just to a boil, simmer for 5 minutes
- Stir in sugar salt and pepper
- Garnish with mint

Serves 4

Baked French Fries

3 medium	Potatoes, approx. 6 to 7 oz each, peeled
3 tsp	Cooking oil
1/3 tsp	Paprika
¼ tsp	Salt

Preheat oven to 425°F

- Cut potatoes lengthwise into ½-inch sticks
- Place sticks in a bowl of ice water to crisp, drain
- Pat dry with paper towels
- Place potato sticks in a plastic bag with cooking oil, paprika, and salt; shake to coat
- On a large baking sheet, arrange the potato strips in a single layer
- Bake for 30 to 35 minutes or until golden, turning once or twice

Serves 4

Turnip Delight

4 cups	Yellow turnips, cooked and mashed
1 cup	Apple sauce, drained
¼ cup	Butter, softened
¼ cup	Brown sugar, packed
1 tsp	Nutmeg
	Salt and pepper to taste
2 Tbsp	Butter
¼ cup	Pecans, finely chopped
½ cup	Panko crumbs (or dry bread crumbs)

Preheat oven to 350°F

- In medium saucepan, heat turnip and apple sauce
- Add ¼ cup butter, brown sugar, nutmeg, salt and pepper
- Stir and taste, adding more salt and pepper if needed
- Turn into a shallow casserole
- Melt 2 Tbsp butter in small saucepan
- Stir in nuts and crumbs and cook stirring until evenly coated with the butter
- Sprinkle mixture over top of turnip and apple sauce
- Bake uncovered at 350°F for 20 minutes or until browned

Serves 4 to 6

Potato Topped Vegetables

Topping:

4	Potatoes, diced
3 Tbsp	Butter
3 Tbsp	Sour cream
4 Tbsp	Parmesan cheese, grated
½ tsp	Salt
Dash	Pepper

- Cook the potatoes in boiling salted water for 10 to 15 minutes or until cooked
- Drain and mash with the butter, sour cream, half of the cheese, salt & pepper

Vegetables:

1 medium	Carrot, peeled and diced
¾ cup	Cauliflower florets
¾ cup	Broccoli florets
1 small	Onion, sliced
½ cup	Sugar snap peas, cut into ½-inch pieces
1/3 cup	Red pepper, cut into ½-inch pieces
3 Tbsp	Butter
¼ cup	Flour
2/3 cup	Vegetable stock
1 1/3 cup	White wine
1 cup	Milk
1 can	Whole mushrooms, cut into quarters

- Cook vegetables in boiling water for about 8 minutes, drain and set aside
- Melt butter in a large saucepan, stir in the flour and cook for 1 to 2 minutes then remove from heat

- Stir in the stock, wine and milk, return to heat and bring to a boil stirring until thickened
- Add vegetables and mushrooms to the sauce, mix gently
- Spoon the vegetable mixture into a 9-inch baking pan
- Spoon the potato mixture on top, covering vegetables completely
- Sprinkle with remaining cheese and bake for 35 to 45 minutes

Serves 4 to 6

French Green Beans

2 pounds	Fresh green beans
1 small clove	Garlic, chopped very fine
¼ cup	Butter
1 tsp	Salt
1/8 tsp	Pepper
2 Tbsp	Parsley, finely chopped

- Wash beans, cook in boiling salted water 7 to 9 minutes or until crisp tender
- Do not overcook or they will go soggy
- Drain beans, add the garlic, butter, salt, pepper and parsley

Serves 6

Baked Mashed Potatoes

8 medium	Potatoes
3 Tbsp	Butter
½ cup	Sour cream
	Salt and pepper to taste
1 cup	White cheddar cheese, grated

Preheat oven to 400°F

- Bake potatoes for 40 to 50 minutes or until soft
- Split lengthwise and scoop out the centres into a mixing bowl
- Set shells aside
- Turn the broiler on to preheat
- Add butter and sour cream to the potatoes then mash until well mixed
- Season with salt and pepper
- Stir in the cheese
- Mound potato mixture into the shells
- Broil 10 inches from the heat until potatoes are heated through

Serves 10 to 12

Stuffed Peppers

1 pound	Ground beef
½ cup	Onion, finely chopped
¼ cup	Fine bread crumbs
¼ cup	Celery, finely chopped
1 large	Egg
¼ tsp	Black pepper
3/4 tsp	Salt
2 tsp	Dried parsley
6 medium	Green peppers

Preheat oven to 350°F

- Mix first 8 ingredients in a large bowl until well blended, set aside
- Wash and dry the peppers
- Cut top ¼ inch off the peppers then scrape out the seeds and membranes
- Save the pepper tops to place on top of filled peppers
- Fill each pepper with the meat mixture, dividing equally, and mounding slightly
- Replace the tops then arrange peppers in a 9 x 13 baking pan
- Bake uncovered at 350°F until tops are browned and meat registers 165°F; approximately one hour

Serves 6

Sauerkraut and Sausage

1 Tbsp	Vegetable oil
1 pound	Bratwurst sausage (casings removed), chopped
2 medium	Apples, peeled and chopped
1 can (28 oz)	Sauerkraut, drained and rinsed
1½ cups	Chicken stock
4	Potatoes, cut into bite size pieces

- Heat oil in large heavy skillet over medium heat
- Add sausage and apple, cook 5 minutes until browned
- Add sauerkraut, stock and potatoes
- Reduce heat to low, cover and simmer for 20 to 30 minutes or until potatoes are fork tender

Serves 4

Curried Sweet Potato Wontons

1 Tbsp	Butter or margarine
1 cup	Sweet potatoes, peeled and diced small
½ cup	Red pepper, diced fine
¼ cup	Green onion, sliced fine
2 tsp	Curry powder
¼ tsp	Salt
1	Egg
2 tsp	Flour
½ cup	Plain yogurt
24	Wonton wrappers
2 Tbsp	Melted butter

Preheat oven to 350°F

- In frying pan melt 1 Tbsp butter, stir in sweet potato, red pepper and onion
- Cook covered over medium heat until potato is tender (3 – 5 minutes)
- Stir in curry powder and salt, cool
- Beat egg and flour together until smooth
- Beat in the yogurt
- Stir in the potato mixture
- Brush one side of wonton wrappers with melted butter
- Press wonton (buttered side up) into muffin tin
- Spoon potato mixture into wonton
- Bake at 350°F for 12 to 15 minutes or until centre is set and wontons are golden

Makes 24

Pasta and Rice

Manicotti

Crepes:

6 large	Eggs
1 tsp	Salt
1½ cup	Flour
1½ cup	Water

Filling:

1 medium	Onion, chopped fine
1 pound each	Ground pork and ground beef
1 tsp	Parsley chopped fine
¼ tsp	Black pepper
1 tsp each	Salt, garlic powder, Italian spice blend
¼ cup	Parmesan cheese, grated
2 – 2¼ cup	Bread crumbs
3	Eggs, beaten
1 large can	Spaghetti sauce
	Mozzarella cheese, grated

Crepes:
- Combine all ingredients in blender, mix well and set aside for ½ hour
- Make crepes using 1 – 2 Tbsp of batter for each one; place in lightly greased fry pan, fry until light brown, turn over and cook 1 – 2 minutes more; set aside until filling is ready

Filling:
- Combine all ingredients, except spaghetti sauce and mix well
- Cover bottom of casserole dish with about 1 cup of spaghetti sauce
- For each manicotti use 1 – 1½ Tbsp mixture, form into sausage shapes and roll up inside one crepe

- Place manicotti into casserole dish and sprinkle with Parmesan cheese
- Lightly cover manicotti with remaining spaghetti sauce
- Sprinkle with mozzarella cheese and bake for 1 hour at 350 °F

Serves 8 to 10

Chinese Fried Rice

¼ cup	Vegetable oil
2 cups	Rice
¾ cup	Green onions, sliced
4 cups	Chicken stock
1/8 tsp	Dry mustard
2 Tbsp	Soy sauce
¼ cup	Oyster sauce
¼ cup	Vegetable oil
½ cup	Canned sliced mushrooms
¾ cup	Peas, cooked

- Heat the oil in a wok or deep frying pan over medium heat
- Add the rice and stir fry until the rice is golden
- Add the onions and stir fry until onions are limp
- Add the stock, mustard, soy sauce, oyster sauce, vegetable oil and mushrooms; turn the heat to low
- Cover and cook for about 15 to 20 minutes until rice is cooked
- Add peas and heat through

Serves 10 to 12

Rice and Cheese Sauce

Rice:

2 cups	Water
1 cup	Long grained rice
1 tsp	Salt
¼ cup	Butter
1 small	Red pepper, finely chopped
1 small	Green pepper finely chopped

- Combine water, rice and salt in saucepan, bring to a boil
- Lower heat, cover and cook until rice is cooked approx. 15 to 20 minutes
- Place cooked rice into a mixing bowl; add the butter and stir until butter melts
- Stir in the peppers and mix well
- Press the rice mixture into an oiled mold, let stand 15 to 20 minutes then invert on to a serving dish

Sauce:

3 Tbsp	Butter
3 Tbsp	Flour
2 cups	Milk
¾ tsp	Salt
¼ tsp	Pepper
1 cup	Parmesan cheese

- Melt butter, add flour and stir well
- Add milk, salt and pepper and cook stirring until thick
- Add the parmesan cheese and stir until it melts
- Pour over the rice and serve

Serves 6

Pasta and Beans

2 Tbsp	Olive oil
3 cloves	Garlic, crushed
1 small	Onion, chopped
2 Tbsp	Basil, chopped
1 pound	Green beans, cut into 2-inch pieces
1 can	Tomato sauce
2 cups	Vegetable broth
½ cup	Red wine
	Salt and pepper to taste
1 pound	Penne pasta
2 Tbsp	Butter
	Grated parmesan cheese

- Heat 2 Tbsp oil in large fry pan; sauté the garlic and onion about 3 minutes or until soft but not browned
- Add basil, beans, tomato sauce, vegetable broth and wine
- Season with salt and pepper, stir well, cover and cook for 10 minutes or until beans are tender
- Remove lid and cook another five minutes or until sauce is a little thick
- In another pot, bring water to a boil
- Add the penne and cook for about eight minutes or until tender; drain then return to sauce pan
- Add the butter and stir until butter melts
- Serve the beans with the hot buttered pasta and sprinkle with grated parmesan cheese

Serves 4

Pasta and Broccoli

5 cups	Water
4 envelopes	Vegetable bouillon
4 tsp	Salt
4 cups	Macaroni
6	Green onions, chopped
1½ cups	Broccoli florets
2 Tbsp	Butter
½ cup	Parmesan cheese, grated

- Mix water and bouillon, and salt in large pot and bring to a boil
- Add macaroni, boil for seven minutes
- Add onion and broccoli and boil three to four minutes longer
- Drain add butter and cheese, mix well

Serves 4

Gnocchi (Potato Dumplings)

4 - 3½" to 4"	Potatoes, diced
1	Egg yolk
1 tsp	Olive oil
1 cup	Flour
	Salt and pepper

- Cook potatoes until tender, drain and mash
- Transfer potatoes to a lightly floured chopping board and make a well in the centre
- Add the egg yolk, olive oil and a little of the flour to potatoes
- Quickly mix together adding more flour as needed until a firm dough forms
- Divide the mixture into small balls and roll out in to ¾-inch diameter ropes
- Cut each rope into 1-inch pieces and roll each piece off the back of a floured fork. Pieces will curl up a little. If fork gets sticky, dip it in more flour
- Cook gnocchi in boiling salted water until they rise to the top of the water. Do not overcook. Drain and serve with tomato sauce and parmesan cheese

Serves 4

Tomato Sauce

2 Tbsp	Olive oil
¼ cup each	Onion, green pepper, and celery, diced
12 oz	Tomato sauce
½ tsp	Italian spice mix
	Salt and pepper to taste

- Heat oil in a saucepan
- Add the onion, pepper and celery; cook for about six minutes
- Add tomato sauce, Italian spice mix, salt and pepper to taste
- Cook five to six minutes
- Pour over the cooked and drained gnocchi

Serves 4

Homemade Ravioli

Pasta

1½ cup	Flour
½ tsp	Salt
1 Tbsp	Olive oil
2	Eggs, beaten

- Sift flour and salt into a food processor; with the machine running, trickle in the oil and eggs and blend to a stiff, smooth dough
- Allow the machine to run for at least two minutes
- Divide the dough into an even number of balls and roll each out on a lightly floured surface to a thickness of about ¼ inch
- Fold the pasta into three and re-roll; repeating this step up to six times until the dough is smooth and no longer sticky;

rolling the pasta slightly more thinly each time. Final roll should be about 1/8 inch thick
- Keep the rolled dough under clean, dry towels until ready to fill

Filling

1	Small onion, small carrot, small green pepper, all chopped fine
1 Tbsp	Olive oil
¼ cup	Ricotta cheese
3 Tbsp	Grated parmesan cheese
½ Tbsp	Dried basil
	Salt and pepper to taste

- Fry onion, green pepper and carrots in oil for five minutes; cool
- Mix cheeses, basil and salt and pepper together; add to cooled vegetables
- Lay out one sheet of pasta and place small scoops of filling in neat rows; about 2-inches apart
- Brush between filling with a little water; place another pasta sheet on top
- Press down firmly between the rows then cut with a pastry cutter
- If the edges pop open press back with your fingers
- Leave ravioli to dry then boil in plenty of salted water for 5 minutes
- Drain then toss in a little oil before serving with the tomato sauce

Serves 6

Perogies

2	Eggs, beaten
1¼ cup	Lukewarm water
6 cups	Flour
1 tsp	Salt
1 cup	Butter
3 Tbsp	Sour cream

- Add the eggs to the warm water then add all remaining ingredients
- Knead mixture until smooth then let rest for ½ to 1 hour
- Roll out dough approximately 1/8 inch thick and cut into circles (2½")
- Place filling on half of each circle, fold over and seal edges with water
- Boil perogies in salted water until they rise to the top
- Remove from water with a strainer, serve with sour cream

Serves 6 to 8

Filling

5 medium	Potatoes, peeled and cut into large cubes
2½ Tbsp	Butter
	Salt and pepper to taste
½ cup	Cheddar cheese, shredded

- Boil potatoes until done; drain
- Add butter, salt and pepper then mash
- Add the cheese and mix well
- Fill perogies as noted above

Serves 6 to 8

Breads and Buns

Norwegian Whole Wheat Bread

2 pkg	Yeast
1/3 cup	Warm water
3 cups	White flour, sifted
3 cups	Whole wheat flour
2 cups	Buttermilk
1½ tsp	Salt
2/3 cup	Molasses
1/3 cup	Butter, melted

- Dissolve yeast in the warm water.
- Mix together the white and whole wheat flours, set aside
- Heat buttermilk in a saucepan over low heat just until warm then add the salt, molasses, melted butter and dissolved yeast; blend together
- Gradually stir in the flours; work into the dough until it is quite stiff
- Turn dough out on to a floured board and knead until smooth and elastic
- Place in buttered bowl, cover and let rise until doubled, about 1½ hours
- When doubled, punch down and turn it out onto a floured board
- Divide dough into two parts, shape each into a loaf; place in buttered pan
- Cover and let rise again until doubled; about 1¼ hours
- Brush tops of loaves with melted butter
- Bake at 350°F for 45 minutes or until browned and done

Makes 2 loaves

Whole Wheat Bread

1 Tbsp	Sugar
¾ cup	Luke warm water
3 pkg	Yeast
3¾ cup	Milk
¾ cup	Sugar
4 Tbsp	Shortening
4½ tsp	Salt
10 cups	Whole wheat flour, unsifted

- Dissolve 1 Tbsp sugar in water, add yeast; let foam up
- Scald milk. Add sugar and shortening and salt
- Stir to dissolve and cool to lukewarm.
- Add yeast when liquid is lukewarm
- Stir in 6 cups flour; beat until smooth and elastic
- Work in 4 more cups of flour
- Turn out on a floured board and knead until light and smooth
- Place in greased bowl, cover, let rise until double in bulk; about 1½ hours
- Turn out on a floured board, knead for 10 minutes
- Shape into loaves, place in buttered loaf pans and let rise until double in bulk
- Bake at 375°F for 40 to 50 minutes or until done

Makes 3 loaves

Irish Soda Bread

4 cups	Flour
1 tsp	Salt
1 tsp	Sugar
1 tsp	Baking soda
1½ cups	Buttermilk

Preheat oven to 350°F

- Sift the dry ingredients into a bowl
- Make a hollow in the centre and pour in one cup of the buttermilk
- Mix with your hands and add enough additional buttermilk to make a firm, but not dry, dough
- Turn onto a floured board and knead gently
- Shape into a round loaf
- Make a cut across the top so that it will not crack
- Place on a buttered baking pan and bake for 40 to45 minutes in 350°F oven

Makes 1 round loaf

Baking Powder Biscuits

2 cups	Flour
3 tsp	Baking powder
½ tsp	Salt
¼ cup	Butter
¾ cup	Milk

Preheat oven to 450°F

- Combine the flour, baking powder and salt
- Cut in the butter until you have a mixture the consistency of course meal
- Stir in the milk; using only enough so that the dough holds together and can be kneaded
- Turn the dough onto a floured board and knead lightly about 8 - 10 times
- Roll out to ½ inch thickness and cut into 2-inch rounds
- Bake on an ungreased cookie sheet at 450°F for 12 to 15 minutes

Makes 12 biscuits

Cheese Bread

2 pkg	Yeast
½ cup	Warm water
6 cups	Flour
1 Tbsp	Sugar
1 tsp	Salt
2/3 cup	Butter
2 cups	Cheddar cheese, shredded
1¼ cups	Cold mashed potatoes
4 large	Eggs
½ cup	Scalded milk

Preheat oven to 375°F

- Dissolve the yeast in the water
- Sift the flour, sugar and salt together
- Combine the yeast mixture, butter, cheese, potatoes, eggs and milk; beat until blended
- Add the dry ingredients; thoroughly mix together
- Turn onto a floured board and knead for 6 minutes.
- Place in a buttered bowl, cover and let rise until doubled
- Punch down and knead again for about 3 minutes
- Shape into 2 loaves
- Place into well-buttered loaf pans
- Cover and let rise until doubled
- Bake at 375°F for 35 to 40 minutes

Makes 2 loaves

Feather Buns

1 pkg	Yeast
¼ cup	Water, lukewarm
1 tsp	Sugar
2 cups	Milk, scalded
½ cup	Butter
1½ Tbsp	Sugar
1½ tsp	Salt
2	Eggs, well beaten
4 cups	Flour, sifted

Preheat oven to 425°F

- Mix together yeast, ¼ cup water and 1 tsp sugar; let stand for 10 minutes
- Put butter, sugar, salt and milk in a large bowl; stir until butter melts and liquid is lukewarm
- When yeast has risen, add mixture to lukewarm milk mixture; stir well
- Add the well beaten eggs and flour
- Place in an electric mixer bowl and beat really well (beating really well is important for the rising of these buns)
- Cover and place the dough in a warm place and let rise until doubled about 1½ hours
- Beat the batter again
- Spoon into greased muffin pans
- Let rise again for about 30 to 40 minutes
- Bake at 425°F for 10 to 15 minutes or until done

Makes 1 dozen

Cheese Wafers

½ pound	Cheddar cheese, grated
½ cup	Butter
½ tsp	Salt
1¼ cup	Flour
1/8 tsp	Dry basil
1/8 tsp	Garlic salt

Preheat oven to 350°F

- Combine all ingredients in medium bowl and work together until smooth
- Shape into a roll and wrap in waxed paper; chill
- Slice 1/8" thick; as you would refrigerator cookies
- Places on a buttered cookie sheet
- Bake at 350°F for 10 minutes or until lightly brown and done

Makes approximately 1 dozen

Welsh Cakes

¾ cup	Shortening
¾ cup	Sugar
½ tsp	Salt
1	Egg, beaten
3 cups	Flour
3 tsp	Baking powder
1 cup	Currants
¾ cup	Milk

- Cream the shortening, sugar, and salt
- Add the egg and mix well
- Combine the flour, baking powder and currants in separate bowl
- Add the milk mixture alternately with the flour mixture to make a soft dough
- Roll the dough quite thinly on a floured board
- Cut into circles or squares and bake on a hot griddle or in a heavy fry pan

Makes 1 dozen

Yeast Buns

2 pkg	Yeast
½ cup	Warm water
2 tsp	Sugar
1½ cup	Warm water
¾ cup	Vegetable oil
½ cup	Sugar
1 tsp	Salt
3	Eggs, well beaten
5 to 6 cups	Flour

Preheat oven to 375°F

- Combine yeast, ½ cup warm water, and sugar; let stand until it bubbles up
- Combine the 1½ cup warm water, vegetable oil, sugar and salt
- Add the well beaten eggs
- Add the yeast mixture
- Add flour a little at a time until you have a soft dough
- Place in a greased bowl and cover until doubled
- Punch down and let rise again
- Place in greased muffin tin
- Bake at 375°F for 20 minutes

Makes 1 dozen

Note: can be made into 1 loaf, baked for 35 to 40 minutes at 375°F

MORE SHARE WITH LOVE CANADIAN COOKING

Angel Buns

2 pkg	Yeast
¼ cup	Warm water
2 cups	Warm buttermilk
5 cups	Flour
1/3 cup	Sugar
1 Tbsp	Baking powder
1 tsp	Baking soda
2 tsp	Salt
1 cup	Shortening
	Melted butter

Preheat oven to 450°F

- Dissolve yeast in warm water, let stand 5 minutes; stir in buttermilk then set aside
- In a large mixing bowl, combine flour, sugar, baking powder, soda and salt
- Cut in shortening with a pastry blender until mixture resembles coarse meal
- Stir in yeast buttermilk mixture; mix well
- Turn out onto a lightly floured board; knead lightly 3 or 4 times
- Roll to ½ inch thickness; cut with a cookie cutter
- Place the rolls on a greased pan
- Cover and let rise about 2 hours
- Bake at 450°F for 10 to 12 minutes
- Brush the tops with melted butter

Makes about 30 buns

Cookies

Jam Jams

1 cup	Brown sugar
1 cup	Shortening
2	Eggs, beaten
6 Tbsp	Corn syrup
1 tsp	Vanilla
2 tsp	Baking soda
¼ tsp	Salt
3 – 4 cups	Flour

Preheat oven to 375°F

- Cream sugar and shortening till fluffy
- Add well beaten eggs, syrup and vanilla
- Sift soda and flour together then gradually beat in to egg/ sugar mixture until mixture is stiff enough to roll
- Chill dough for ½ hour
- Roll out dough to ¼ inch thickness
- Cut into circles
- Bake in hot oven 375 °F for 10 to 15 minutes
- Cool cookies
- Sandwich cookies together with date filling or jam

Makes about 2 dozen

Snow Balls

½ cup	Margarine or butter, melted
3 Tbsp	Cocoa
3 Tbsp	Cold coffee
1 – 2 Tbsp	Vanilla
1 cup	Sugar
2½ cups	Rolled oats
	Coconut, fine unsweetened

- Knead all ingredients together
- Form into balls, approx. 1" diameter
- Roll in fine coconut

Makes about 1½ to 2 dozen

Grans Coconut Cookies

1 cup	Margarine or butter
½ cup	Brown sugar
½ cup	White sugar
1	Egg
1 tsp	Almond extract
2 cups	Flour
1 tsp	Baking soda
1 tsp	Cream of tartar
1 cup	Fine coconut

Preheat oven to 300 °F

- Cream margarine and the sugars until fluffy
- Add egg and almond extract, mix well
- Mix dry ingredients and coconut together
- Add to margarine/sugar mixture
- Roll in to 1-inch balls and place onto parchment lined cookie sheet
- Press with a fork
- Bake at 300 °F for 20 – 25 minutes

Makes about 2 dozen

Meringue Shells

4	Egg whites
1 cup	Sugar
1 Tbsp	Lemon juice

Preheat oven to 250°F

- Beat egg whites until foamy
- Gradually add the sugar a tablespoon at a time; beating thoroughly after each addition
- Continue to beat until the meringue forms sharp peaks when the beater is raised
- Add the lemon juice and continue beating until the meringue again forms sharp peaks
- On a cookie sheet lined with parchment paper, shape with a spoon into nests or rounds
- Allow about 2 inches space between shells
- Bake at 250°F for one hour and 20 minutes until the shells are thoroughly dried and the tops are cream coloured

Makes 12 medium shells

If making nests, after baking they can be filled with jam, jelly or fruit

Coconut Crisps

1 cup	Butter
1½ cup	Sugar
2	Eggs, well beaten
½ tsp	Vanilla
1 cup	Fine coconut
2 cups	Flour
2 tsp	Baking powder

Preheat oven to 350°F

- Cream butter and sugar until fluffy; add well beaten egg
- Add vanilla and coconut
- In separate bowl, sift flour and baking powder; add to the butter mixture
- Drop from a spoon onto a greased cookie sheet
- Bake at 350°F for 10 to 15 minutes

Makes 1½ to 2 dozen

Orange Date Cookies

2 cups	Flour
½ tsp	Salt
1 tsp	Baking soda
1 tsp	Cinnamon
1 tsp	Nutmeg
1 cup	Oatmeal
¾ cup	Shortening
1 cup	Brown sugar
2	Eggs
2 Tbsp	Orange juice
1½ Tbsp	Orange rind
1 cup	Chopped dates
¾ cup	Chopped dried apricots

Preheat oven to 375°F

- In a mixing bowl, sift together flour, salt, baking soda, cinnamon, nutmeg; then add the oatmeal
- In separate bowl cream the shortening, gradually add the brown sugar creaming well
- Add the eggs, orange juice and orange rind; mix well
- Blend the dry ingredients gradually in to the creamed mixture mixing thoroughly
- Add the dates and apricots; mix well
- Drop by rounded teaspoonsful onto a greased cookie sheet
- Flatten slightly with a fork
- Bake at 375°F for 10 to 12 minutes

Makes about 3 dozen

Carrot Cookies

1 cup	Shortening
¾ cup	Sugar
1 cup	Carrots, cooked and mashed
1	Egg
1 tsp	Vanilla
3 cups	Flour
2 tsp	Baking powder
½ tsp	Salt
¾ cup	Fine, unsweetened coconut

Preheat oven to 350°F

- Cream shortening and sugar
- Add carrots, egg and vanilla; mix well
- Sift flour, baking powder and salt together and add to carrot mixture
- Stir in coconut
- Drop by teaspoon 2 inches apart
- Bake at 350°F for 20 minutes

Makes 1½ dozen

Sesame Cookies

1 cup	Sesame seeds
½ cup	Fine, unsweetened coconut,
2 cups	Flour
1 tsp	Baking powder
½ tsp	Baking soda
½ tsp	Salt
¾ cup	Butter
1 cup	Brown sugar, firmly packed
1	Egg
1 tsp	Vanilla

Preheat oven to 350°F

- Toast the sesame seeds and coconut in a 350°F oven until light brown; set aside
- In a medium bowl, sift the flour, baking powder, baking soda and salt
- In separate bowl cream the butter and brown sugar well
- Add the egg, vanilla, sesame seeds and coconut; beat well
- Gradually add dry ingredients, mixing thoroughly
- Drop rounded teaspoons on to a cookie sheet; flatten to 1/8 inch thick
- Bake 10 to 12 minutes at 350°F

Makes about 4 dozen

Heirloom Cookies

½ cup	Butter
½ cup	Shortening
1 cup	Icing sugar
½ tsp	Salt
1¼ cups	Ground almonds
2 cups	Flour, sifted
1 Tbsp	Water
1 Tbsp	Vanilla
	Icing sugar for rolling

Preheat oven to 325°F

- Cream together butter and shortening; add the sugar and salt and cream well
- Blend in the ground almonds
- Gradually mix in the flour until thoroughly mixed in
- Add the water and vanilla; mix well with a fork
- Shape into balls using one level tablespoon of dough for each cookie
- Place on ungreased cookie sheet
- Bake at 325°F for 12 to 15 minutes
- Roll in icing sugar while still warm

Makes about 4 dozen

Coconut Cookies

1¼ cups	Flour, sifted
½ tsp	Baking powder
½ tsp	Salt
½ cup	Butter
½ cup	Sugar
1	Egg
½ tsp	Vanilla
1 cup	Fine, unsweetened coconut
½ cup	Walnuts, chopped

Preheat oven to 375°F

- Combine flour, baking powder and salt; set aside
- In separate bowl, combine butter and sugar; cream well
- Add egg and vanilla; mix well
- Add dry ingredients and blend thoroughly
- Mix in the coconut and walnuts
- Drop by level tablespoon on to a greased cookie sheet
- Bake at 375°F for 10 to 12 minutes

Makes about 2½ dozen

Macadamia Chocolate Chip Cookies

2¼ cups	Flour
1 tsp	Baking soda
½ tsp	Salt
1 cup	Butter or margarine
¾ cup	White sugar
¾ cup	Brown sugar, packed
2 large	Eggs
1½ tsp	Vanilla
2 cups	Chocolate chips
¾ cup	Macadamia nuts (or almonds)
½ cup	Coconut, flaked

Preheat oven to 375 °F

- In separate bowl, combine flour, soda and salt, set aside
- Cream butter and sugars until light and fluffy
- Add eggs one at a time, beating well after each addition
- Stir in vanilla
- Add dry ingredients and beat until well blended
- Stir in chocolate chips, nuts and coconut
- Drop by spoonful on to ungreased baking sheet, about 3" apart
- Bake at 375 °F for 15 – 18 minutes or until golden brown

Makes 2 dozen

Double Chocolate Chip Cookies

1¾ cup	Flour
¼ tsp	Baking soda
1 cup	Butter or margarine at room temp
1 large	Egg
1 tsp	Vanilla
1 cup	White sugar
½ cup	Brown sugar, packed
1/3 cup	Cocoa powder, unsweetened
2 Tbsp	Milk
1 cup	Pecans or walnuts, chopped
1 cup	Chocolate chips

Preheat oven to 350 °F

- Combine flour and baking soda, set aside
- Cream butter well, add egg
- Add vanilla and sugars and beat until fluffy
- At low speed, beat in cocoa powder then milk
- With wooden spoon mix in dry ingredients just until blended
- Stir in nuts and chocolate chips
- Drop dough by rounded teaspoon on to ungreased baking sheets
- Bake at 350 °F for 12 to 13 minutes
- Remove from baking sheets to cool

Makes 4 dozen

Peanut Dimples

3	Egg whites
Pinch	Cream of Tartar
½ cup	Sugar
6	Digestive biscuits, crushed
¼ tsp	Vanilla
½ cup	Salted peanuts

Preheat oven to 300°F

- Beat egg whites and cream of tartar until stiff
- Add sugar and beat until dissolved
- Fold in crushed digestive biscuits, vanilla and peanuts
- Drop by teaspoonful on to foil-lined baking tray
- Bake at 300°F for 15 – 20 minutes or until crisp

Makes 36

Powder Puffs

2	Egg whites
4 Tbsp	Sugar
2	Egg yolks
¼ cup	Corn starch
1 tsp	Cream of tartar
2 Tbsp	Flour
	Jam

Preheat oven to 450°F

- Beat egg whites until stiff, gradually add sugar
- Add egg yolks one at a time beating well after each addition
- Combine cornstarch, cream of tartar, and flour and fold in to egg mixture
- Drop ½ tsp at a time on to greased baking trays
- Bake at 450°F for 5 to 6 minutes
- Cool, then join in pairs with jam
- Dust with icing sugar

Makes about 16

Best Oatmeal Cookies

1 cup	Light or dark raisins
2/3 cup	Shortening
1½ cup	Sugar
2	Eggs, beaten
½ cup	Milk
1 tsp	Vanilla
2 cups	Flour
½ tsp	Baking soda
1 tsp	Salt
1 tsp	Baking powder
1 tsp	Cinnamon
2½ cups	Quick-cooking rolled oats

Preheat oven to 350°F

- Rinse and drain raisins
- Cream shortening and sugar together thoroughly
- Stir in beaten eggs, milk, vanilla and raisins
- Sift together flour, baking soda, salt, baking powder and cinnamon
- Add oats to dry ingredients
- Stir dry mixture into creamed mixture, mixing thoroughly
- Drop by teaspoonful onto greased baking sheet
- Bake at 350 °F for 12 – 15 minutes

Makes about 5 dozen

Key Lime Meltaways

¾ cup	Butter, at room temperature
1 cup	Icing sugar
	Grated zest from 4 tiny or 2 large limes
2 Tbsp	Freshly squeezed lime juice
1 Tbsp	Vanilla
2 cups	Flour
2 Tbsp	Cornstarch
¼ tsp	Salt

Preheat oven to 350°F

- Cream butter and 1/3 cup of sugar until fluffy
- Add lime zest, lime juice and vanilla, beat until fluffy
- In separate bowl whisk together flour, cornstarch and salt. Add to butter mixture and beat on low until combined
- Roll dough into ½ to ¾ inch diameter ropes then wrap in parchment
- Chill at least one hour
- Heat oven to 350 °F
- Line two baking sheets with parchment
- Remove parchment from the dough, cut dough into 2-inch pieces
- Place on baking sheets 1 inch apart
- Bake until barely golden, about 12 – 15 minutes, cool slightly on wire rack
- Place remaining 2/3 cup icing sugar in a plastic bag
- While still warm, toss cookies in icing sugar in the plastic bag

Note: Regular limes work well for these cookies but Key limes make them more special

Makes approximately 5 dozen

Never Fail Cream Puffs

½ cup	Water
¼ tsp	Salt
¼ cup	Butter
½ cup	Flour, sifted
2	Eggs

Preheat oven to 425 °F

- Bring water to a boil in medium saucepan
- Add salt and butter then bring to a boil again
- Add flour all at once and stir vigorously until mixture forms a stiff ball
- Remove from heat
- Add eggs one at a time, beating well after each addition until mixture is smooth (an electric mixer is helpful)
- Shape puffs by dropping from a tablespoon onto a greased 17 x 11 inch baking sheet
- Bake in preheated oven at 425 °F for 15 minutes
- Reduce heat to 375 °F and bake 25 minutes longer
- Split and fill with sweetened whipped cream

Makes 6 large puffs

Soft Breakfast Cookies

1¼ cup	Milk
1 cup	Oil
2	Eggs
2 tsp	Vanilla
¾ cup	White sugar
1 cup	Brown sugar, packed
4 cups	Oatmeal
3 cups	Flour
2 tsp	Baking soda
2 tsp	Salt
2 tsp	Cinnamon
1 cup	Either craisins, chocolate chips, coconut, nuts, raisins

Preheat oven to 350°F

- Mix all wet ingredients together then add the sugars
- Mix until well blended
- Stir in oats, flour, baking soda, salt and cinnamon
- Mix until blended
- Add craisins, chocolate chips, coconut, nuts and/or raisins
- Drop by large spoonfulls onto parchment lined cookie sheet
- Bake at 350°F for 15 to 20 minutes
- They will spring back like little cakes when done

Makes approximately 30 large cookies

Cakes

Happy Day Cake

½ cup	Shorting
2½ cups	Cake flour
1½ cups	White sugar
3 tsp	Baking powder
1 tsp	Salt
1 cup	Milk
2	Eggs
1 tsp	Vanilla

Preheat oven to 375 °F

- Cream shortening until fluffy
- Sift together flour, sugar, baking powder and salt
- Add dry ingredients to shortening
- Add ¾ of the milk and beat for two minutes
- Add eggs, vanilla and the rest of the milk; beat for one minute
- Pour into two 8" layer pans
- Bake at 375 °F for 25 to 30 minutes or until toothpick comes out dry

Serves 10 to 12

Petite Fours

2¼ cups	Cake flour
3 tsp	Baking powder
½ tsp	Salt
1¼ cups	Sugar
1¼ cups	Whipping cream
4	Egg whites
1 tsp	Vanilla

Preheat oven to 350°F

- Sift together flour, baking powder, salt and sugar; set aside
- In separate bowl, beat the whipping cream until thick
- Add the sifted dry ingredients, the unbeaten egg whites and vanilla
- Beat in mixer at low speed until the batter is blended
- Then beat on medium speed for 2 minutes
- Pour batter into well-greased and lightly floured 13 x 9 x 2 inch pan
- Bake at 350°F for 35 to 40 minutes
- Cool 10 to 15 minutes before removing from pan; cool thoroughly
- When cool, cut with a sharp knife into small squares or any shape desired
- Frost with icing and decorate with coloured sugar, candied fruit or nuts
- See recipe for frosting on next page

Makes about 2½ dozen

Frosting for Petite Fours

2 cups	Sugar
1 cup	Water
1/8 tsp	Cream of tartar
2 cups	Icing sugar

- Combine sugar, water and cream of tartar in medium pot
- Cook over direct until it reaches 226°F or to a thin syrup
- Stir ONLY until the sugar dissolves
- Remove from heat and pour into the top of a double boiler
- Cool until lukewarm
- Place icing sugar in a bowl and gradually add warm sugar mixture until mixture pours easily
- Place a few cakes in rows on a wire rack over a cookie sheet allowing space between the cakes
- Pour frosting over the cakes covering the tops and sides allowing the frosting to drip onto the cookie sheet
- Scrape frosting from cookie sheet, reheat over hot water and use for other cakes
- Repeat until all the cakes are coated

Sponge Cake

1 cup	Flour
1½ tsp	Baking powder
4 large	Eggs
1 cup	Butter, very soft
1 cup	Sugar
1 tsp	Vanilla
	Icing sugar for dusting
	Jam

Preheat oven to 350°F

- Grease two 8-inch cake pans and line with parchment paper, set aside
- Sift the flour and baking powder into a bowl
- Add the eggs, butter, sugar and vanilla
- With electric mixer on medium speed, beat together until you have a smooth, well-combined mixture 1 to 2 minutes
- Divide the batter between the two 8-inch cake pans
- Bake at 350°F for 30 to 35 minutes (do not open oven for at least 30 minutes)
- Cool for about 10 minutes before removing from the pans
- Carefully peel off the parchment paper then cool completely on wire rack
- Spread one layer with jam then place the other layer on top
- Dust with icing sugar

Serves 10 to 12

Chocolate Zucchini Cake

2½ cup	Flour, unsifted
½ cup	Cocoa
2½ tsp	Baking powder
1½ tsp	Baking soda
1 tsp	Salt
1 tsp	Cinnamon
1 cup	Chopped nuts
¾ cup	Butter
1½ cups	Sugar
3	Eggs
1 tsp	Vanilla
2 tsp	Grated orange peel
2 cups	Zucchini grated
½ cup	Milk

Preheat oven to 350°F

- Combine the dry ingredients and the chopped nuts, mix well then set aside
- In separate bowl, beat the butter and sugar together until smooth
- Add the eggs one at a time beating well after each addition
- Stir in vanilla, orange peel and zucchini
- Alternately stir the dry ingredients and the milk into zucchini mixture
- Pour batter into a greased and floured 9 x 13 pan
- Bake at 350°F for 45 minutes

Serves 10 to 12

Carrot Pineapple Cake

1½ cups	Flour
1 cup	Sugar
1 tsp	Baking soda
1 tsp	Cinnamon
½ tsp	Salt
2/3 cup	Vegetable oil
2	Eggs
1 cup	Carrots, shredded
½ cup	Crushed pineapple with juice
1 tsp	Baking powder
1 tsp	vanilla

Preheat oven to 350°F

- Combine all ingredients until moistened
- Beat with electric mixer at medium speed for 2 minutes
- Pour into a greased 9 x 9 x 2 inch pan
- Bake at 350°F for 35 to 40 minutes

Serves 8 to 10

Christmas Cake

¾ cup	Butter, softened
¾ cup	Brown sugar
6 large	Eggs
2 cups	Flour
¼ tsp	Salt
1 tsp	Allspice
1 cup	Dark raisins, rinsed
2 cups	Sultana raisins, rinsed
1 cup	Currants, rinsed
¾ cup	Mixed peel (optional)
¾ cup	Glazed cherries, chopped
½ cup	Almonds, blanched and chopped
2 Tbsp	Molasses
1/3 cup	Brandy

Preheat oven to 275°F

- Cream the butter and sugar until soft; then beat in the eggs one at a time
- Combine the flour, salt and allspice then fold into the creamed mixture
- Mix in the remaining ingredients
- Spoon into a greased and lined cake pan
- Bake at 275°F for 6½ hours
- Cool completely then wrap in foil and store in an airtight container for at least 3 weeks

Makes one 9-inch cake

Note: a pan of water on the bottom rack of the oven helps prevent cake from cracking

Easy Cake

1 cup	Flour, sifted
2 tsp	Baking powder
1 tsp	Baking soda
¾ tsp	Salt
½ cup	Unsalted butter, softened
¾ cup	Sugar
2	Eggs, separated
1 tsp	Vanilla
¼ cup	Milk

Preheat oven to 350 °F

- Sift flour, baking powder, baking soda and salt together, set aside
- Cream butter and sugar until light and fluffy
- Add in the egg yolks, vanilla, plus 1 tsp of the flour mixture, beat well
- Add remaining flour mixture and the milk, mix well
- In separate bowl, beat egg whites until they stand in peaks
- Cut and fold egg whites into cake mixture
- Divide mixture between two 8" cake pans
- Bake at 350 °F for 25 – 30 minutes
- Cool slightly before turning out on a wire rack, cool completely

Serves 10 to 12

Frosting: 6 cups icing sugar
            1 cup butter softened
            4 to 6 Tbsp milk
            1½ tsp vanilla

Combine all ingredients, beat at medium speed until fluffy and spread over cooled cake

Pound Cake

1 cup	White sugar
3¼ cups	Flour
4 tsp	Baking powder
¾ tsp	Salt
1 cup	Butter, softened
5	Eggs
1 tsp	Lemon zest, finely grated

Preheat oven to 325 °F

- Mix all the ingredients together and beat well
- Pour batter into greased loaf pan
- Bake at 325 °F for one hour or until firm to touch and leaves sides of pan

Serves 8 to 10

Note: This cake can also be made in a food processor using the all-in-one method. Allow it to be beaten well for 10 minutes or so.

Holiday Mincemeat Cake

½ cup	Brown sugar, firmly packed
1 cup	White sugar
½ cup	Softened butter
2	Eggs
2 tsp	Lemon rind
2 cups	Flour, sifted
1½ tsp	Baking powder
½ tsp	Baking soda
½ tsp	Nutmeg
½ tsp	Allspice
½ tsp	Cinnamon
1/8 tsp	Ground cloves
1 tsp	Salt
1 cup	Evaporated milk, undiluted
1½ cups	Mincemeat
½ cup	Walnuts, chopped

Preheat oven to 350°F

- Mix sugars, butter, eggs and lemon rind until smooth and creamy
- Sift flour, baking powder, baking soda, spices and salt together,
- Add dry ingredients to sugar mixture alternately with evaporated milk beginning and ending with dry ingredients
- Stir in mincemeat and walnuts
- Turn in to a greased 9 x 13 x 2 pan
- Bake at 350°F until done, about 45 – 55 minutes
- Cool 10 minutes
- Sprinkle with sifted icing sugar
- Serve warm or cold

Serves 10 to 12

Best Ever Walnut Squares

Base

1 cup	Flour
2 Tbsp	Brown sugar
½ cup	Butter, softened

Filling

1 cup	Walnuts, chopped
1 cup	Brown sugar
½ cup	Unsweetened coconut
2	Eggs, lightly beaten
1 tsp	Vanilla

Icing

½ cup	Cream cheese, softened
¼ cup	Butter, at room temperature
6 oz	White chocolate, melted until completely smooth
¼ cup	Icing sugar
1 Tbsp	Lemon juice

Preheat oven to 325°F

- Lightly grease a 9-inch square cake pan
- Mix ingredients for the base together to make fine crumbs
- Press into cake pan; bake at 325 °F until cooked through, about 15 minutes
- Meanwhile, stir together filling ingredients
- When base comes out of oven, spread filling over the top
- Return to oven; bake until set, about 25 minutes; cool completely on rack
- Prepare the icing by beating the cream cheese, butter and melted chocolate until smooth

- Gradually beat in the icing sugar and the lemon juice.
- Chill until spreadable, about 10 minutes
- Spread the icing over the cooled walnut filling and cut into diamonds

Makes approximately 16 squares

Nanaimo Bars

Bottom Layer

¼ cup	Butter
¼ cup	White sugar
5 Tbsp	Cocoa
1 tsp	Vanilla
1	Egg
2 cups	Graham wafer crumbs (approx. 28 crackers)
1 cup	Coconut; fine, unsweetened
½ cup	Chopped walnuts

Middle Layer

¼ cup	Butter
5 Tbsp	Milk
2 Tbsp	Vanilla custard powder
2 cups	Icing sugar

Top Layer

4 squares	Semi-sweet chocolate
1 Tbsp	butter

Bottom Layer
- In top of double boiler mix ¼ cup butter, sugar, cocoa, vanilla and egg
- Place over hot water and stir until mixture resembles custard
- Mix graham crumbs, coconut and walnuts, add to custard
- Press mixture into 8" pan

Middle Layer
- Cream ¼ cup butter
- Add milk, custard powder and icing sugar
- Pour over bottom layer; let stand 15 minutes to firm up

Top Layer
- Melt chocolate, add butter
- Spread over top
- Chill

Serves 10 to 12

Apricot Coconut Bars

½ cup	Butter or margarine
¼ cup	White sugar
1½ cup	Flour, sifted
½ tsp	Baking powder
¼ tsp	Salt
2	Eggs, well beaten
1 cup	Sweetened condensed milk
1 1/3 cup	Flaked coconut
1 cup	Apricots, finely chopped

Preheat oven to 350 °F

- In medium bowl combine butter, sugar and 1 cup of the flour and cut ingredients together until mixture resembles coarse corn meal
- Press pastry evenly on bottom of buttered 9-inch square pan
- Bake at 350 for approximately 25 minutes
- Remove from oven and set aside
- In mixing bowl sift baking powder, salt, and remaining flour
- Stir in beaten eggs, condensed milk, coconut and apricots, mix well
- Spread mixture evenly over baked pastry
- Return to oven
- Bake at 350 °F for 30 – 35 minutes or until top is firm
- Cool in pan
- Cut into bars
- Frost with butter cream icing

Serves 10 to 12

Muffins and Loaves

Ginger Pear Muffins

1/3 cup	Butter, softened
½ cup	Brown sugar, packed
2	Eggs
1/3 cup	Buttermilk
1 tsp	Vanilla
2½ cups	Flour
1 tsp	Baking soda
1 tsp	Baking powder
¼ tsp	Salt
¼ tsp	Ground ginger
2 cups	Pears, peeled and finely diced
¼ cup	Candied ginger, finely chopped

Preheat oven to 375 °F

- In large bowl, beat butter and brown sugar until fluffy
- Beat in eggs one at a time
- Beat in buttermilk and vanilla
- In separate bowl, whisk together flour, baking powder, baking soda, salt and ground ginger
- Stir dry ingredients into egg mixture just until combined
- Fold in pears and candied ginger
- Spoon into 12 greased or paper-lined muffin cups
- Bake at 375 °F for about 25 minutes
- Let cool in pan no rack for 5 minutes
- Remove to rack and let cool completely

Makes 12 muffins

Jelly Muffins

1/3 cup	Shortening
½ cup	Sugar
1	Egg
1½ cup	Flour, sifted
1½ tsp	Baking powder
½ tsp	Salt
¼ tsp	Nutmeg
½ cup	Milk
¼ cup	Jelly (grape, apple or any other)
½ cup	Sugar
1 tsp	Cinnamon
5 Tbsp	Butter, melted

Preheat oven to 350°F

- Combine shortening, sugar and egg; mix well
- In separate bowl, sift together flour, baking powder, salt and nutmeg
- Add dry ingredients and milk alternately to the egg mixture
- Fill small greased muffin tins half full
- Put one teaspoon jelly in the centre of each muffin
- Add more batter until cups are ¾ full
- Bake at 350°F for 20 to 25 minutes or until golden brown
- Combine ½ cup sugar and the cinnamon
- Remove muffins from pans at once and roll in the melted butter then in the mixture of sugar and cinnamon

Makes one dozen muffins

Oatmeal Muffins

1¼ cup	Flour
1 cup	Rolled oats
¼ cup	Brown sugar
3 tsp	Baking powder
½ tsp	Salt
¼ tsp	Cinnamon
¾ cup	Raisins
1	Egg
2 Tbsp	Molasses
¼ cup	Oil
1 cup	Milk
1 tsp	Vanilla

Preheat oven to 400°F

- Combine the first seven ingredients in a large bowl; mix together
- Make a well in the centre
- Beat the egg in a small bowl until frothy; mix in the molasses, oil, milk, and vanilla
- Pour liquids into the centre of the dry ingredients
- Stir only until moistened
- The batter will be lumpy
- Fill greased muffin tins ¾ full
- Bake at 400°F for 20 to 25 minutes
- Let stand 5 to 7 minutes before removing from pan
- Serve warm

Makes one dozen large muffins

Peanut Butter Muffins

2 cups	Flour, sifted
3 tsp	Baking powder
1 tsp	Salt
¼ cup	Sugar
1/3 cup	Peanut butter
2	Eggs, beaten
1 cup	Milk
2 Tbsp	Butter, melted

Preheat oven to 400°F

- Sift dry ingredients together
- Work in peanut butter
- In separate bowl, combine the eggs and milk then pour into peanut butter mixture
- Add the melted butter and stir just enough to moisten
- Fill greased muffin pans 2/3 full and bake at 400°F for 25 minutes

Makes one dozen medium muffins

Blueberry Muffins

1½ cups	Flour, sifted
½ cup	White sugar
2 tsp	Baking powder
½ tsp	Salt
1	Egg, beaten
¼ cup	Salad oil
½ cup	Milk
1¼ cup	Blueberries

Preheat oven to 400°F

- Sift dry ingredients together
- In separate bowl, combine beaten egg, oil and milk
- Add liquids to dry ingredients; stirring just until blended
- Fold in blueberries carefully
- Fill muffin pans 2/3 full
- Bake at 400°F for 25 minutes

Makes one dozen muffins

Muffins

3 cups	Flour
2 tsp	Baking powder
1 tsp	Baking soda
½ tsp	Salt
2 cups	Sugar
1¼ cup	Vegetable oil
4 large	Eggs, lightly beaten
2 cups	Carrots, finely grated
½ cup	Walnuts, chopped
½ cup	Dried cranberries

Preheat oven to 375°F

- In a bowl, combine the flour, baking powder, baking soda and salt; whisk well
- In another bowl, combine the sugar and oil; whisk until smooth; add eggs one at a time, beating well after each addition
- Add dry ingredients and mix until just mixed
- Add the carrots, walnuts and cranberries then fold into the batter
- Spoon into muffin pans, filling each 2/3 full
- Bake at 375°F for 30 to 40 minutes or until a toothpick comes out clean
- Cool slightly, serve warm

Makes 24 muffins

Date Nut Loaf

4 cups	Dates, cut up
2 cups	Boiling water
4 cups	Flour
1 tsp	Salt
½ cup	Shortening
1½cups	Brown sugar, firmly packed
2	Eggs
2 tsp	Baking soda
2 cups	Nuts, chopped (walnuts or pecans)

Preheat oven to 350°F

- Pour boiling water over dates, let stand
- Sift flour with salt in a separate bowl
- Cream shortening and brown sugar until light and fluffy
- Add eggs and beat thoroughly
- Add soda to date mixture then add date mixture and flour to the creamed mixture
- Stir in the nuts
- Pour into two well-greased and floured bread pans or four small loaf pans
- Bake at 350°F for 45 minutes to one hour, depending on the size
- Remove from pan immediately after baking
- Cool on rack

Makes 2 loaves or 4 small loaves

Lemon Bread

½ cup	Shortening
1 cup	Sugar
2	Eggs, beaten
½ cup	Milk
½ tsp	Salt
	Grated rind of one lemon
1½ cups	Flour
1 tsp	Baking powder
	Juice of one lemon
¼ cup	Sugar

Preheat oven to 350°F

- Cream shortening and sugar together, add eggs one at a time, beating well
- Add milk, salt and lemon rind
- In separate bowl, combine flour and baking powder
- Add flour to creamed mixture slowly, beating well after each addition
- Bake in a greased loaf pan at 350°F for one hour
- Mix lemon juice and sugar
- Pour over loaf when it comes out of the oven
- Let the juice soak into the loaf

Makes one loaf

Batter Bread

2 to 2½ cups	Flour
3/4 cup	Rolled oats
1 tsp	Salt
1 pkg	Active dry yeast
1 cup	Water
¼ cup	Light molasses
¼ cup	Margarine or butter
1	Egg, beaten

- Grease 8 x 4 loaf pan
- Lightly spoon flour into measuring cup, level off
- In large bowl, combine 1 cup of the flour, rolled oats, salt and yeast; blend well
- In small saucepan, heat water, molasses and margarine to 120 °F to 130 °F
- Add warm liquid and egg to flour mixture
- Blend at low speed until moistened
- Beat for 3 minutes at medium speed
- Stir in remaining 1 to 1½ cups flour to form stiff batter
- Cover loosely with greased plastic wrap and a cloth towel
- Let rise in warm place until light and almost doubled in size (25 – 30 min)
- Stir batter, place in greased loaf pan
- Cover, let rise until batter reaches top of pan (15 -20 min)
- Heat oven to 375 °F
- Uncover dough
- Bake 35 – 40 minutes or until loaf sounds hollow when lightly tapped
- Remove from loaf pan immediately
- Cool on wire rack

Makes 1 – 16 slice loaf

Pastries and Desserts

Butter Tarts

2	Eggs
1½ cup	Brown sugar
1 tsp	Vanilla
½ cup	Butter
2 cups	Raisins
Pinch	Salt
	Purchased tart shells

Preheat oven to 350°F

- Combine first six ingredients in bowl, mix well
- Place mixture in the tart shells
- Bake at 350°F for 15 minutes or until done

Serves 12

French Canadian Sugar Pie

1	Unbaked pie shell
¾ cup	Brown sugar
½ cup	White sugar
¾ cup	Cream
¼ cup	Flour
1 tsp	Vanilla
	Chopped walnuts

Preheat oven to 350°F

- Mix all filling ingredients together; pour into unbaked pie shell
- Bake at 350°F for 25 to 30 minutes
- Sprinkle top of pie with chopped walnuts

Makes one small pie

Strawberry Pie

1	Baked pie shell
4 cups	Strawberries
3 Tbsp	Corn starch
½ cup	Sugar
1 Tbsp	Lemon juice
1 cup	Whipping cream
¼ cup	Sugar
1 Tbsp	Vanilla

- Wash and hull the strawberries; set aside 2 cups of the nicest berries
- Crush the remaining 2 cups of berries
- Add cornstarch, sugar and lemon juice to crushed berries
- Cook over low heat stirring constantly until smooth and creamy; cool
- Place whole strawberries in to the pie shell
- Pour cooled strawberry mixture over the berries
- Refrigerate for 2 hours
- When ready to serve, whip the cream with the ¼ cup sugar and the vanilla then spread over the top of the pie

Makes one small pie

Serves 12

Sour Cream Prune Pie

1 cup	Prunes, chopped
4	Egg separated
1 cup	Sugar
1½ cups	Sour cream
1 tsp	Cinnamon
¼ tsp	Cloves
1	Unbaked pie shell

Preheat oven to 425°F

- Cover prunes with cold water, let stand over night
- Cook prunes in same water until tender
- Remove stones and chop fine
- Beat egg yolks slightly with ½ cup of the sugar
- Mix the sour cream, chopped prunes and spice together; add to egg mixture
- Pour into unbaked pie shell
- Bake in 425°F oven for 15 minutes
- Reduce heat to 325°F and continue baking for 30 minutes or until firm
- Cool pie completely
- Beat the egg whites with remaining½ cup sugar to form a meringue
- Pile meringue lightly on the cooled pie
- Brown in a 325°F oven until a pale golden colour

Serves 6 to 8

Lemon Pie

1	Baked pie shell
1 cup	Sugar
3 Tbsp	Corn starch
½ tsp	Salt
1½ cup	Hot water
2	Egg yolks, beaten
	Juice and rind of one lemon

Preheat oven to 375°F

- Combine sugar, corn starch and salt
- Add the hot water slowly and cook in a double boiler until thick
- Add the beaten egg yolks and cook until clear
- Remove from heat and add the lemon rind and juice
- Pour into the baked pie shell and top with meringue

Meringue:

2	Egg whites
4 Tbsp	Sugar
	Pinch of salt

- Beat egg whites until stiff; add sugar gradually
- Continue to beat until mixture stands in peaks
- Beat in the salt
- Spread over the pie
- Bake at 375°F for 12 to 15 minutes until meringue is golden

Serves 6 to 8

Pecan Pie

1	Unbaked pie shell, 9-inch
1/3 cup	Butter
½ cup	Brown sugar, firmly packed
1 cup	Corn syrup
1 tsp	Vanilla
3	Eggs, slightly beaten
1 cup	Chopped pecans

Preheat oven to 450°F

- Cream butter; gradually add brown sugar creaming well
- Add corn syrup and vanilla; mix well
- Add beaten eggs and pecans
- Turn into pastry lined pie pan
- Bake at 450°F for 10 minutes
- Reduce heat to 350°F for 25 minutes

Serves 6 to 8

Pumpkin Ice Cream Pie

1 – 9-inch	Pie shell, baked and chilled
1 quart	Vanilla ice cream, softened
1 cup	Canned pumpkin
¾ cup	Sugar
¾ tsp	Pumpkin pie spice
¼ tsp	Salt
1 cup	Whipping cream, whipped
½ cup	Chopped salted peanuts

- Spoon ice cream into the pie shell; freeze
- Combine pumpkin, sugar, spice and salt; mix well
- Fold in the whipped cream; spoon mixture over ice cream
- Sprinkle with peanuts
- Cover; freeze several hours or overnight

Serves 6 to 8

Apple Crisp

Filling:

½ cup	Brown sugar, packed
2 Tbsp	Flour
1 tsp	Cinnamon
6 cups	Apples, peeled, cored and sliced (about 5 large)

Topping:

½ cup	Brown sugar, packed
1/3 cup	Flour
1/3 cup	Rolled oats
½ tsp	Cinnamon
¼ cup	Butter, softened
1/3 cup	Walnuts, chopped

Preheat oven to 350°F

- In a large bowl, combine brown sugar, flour and cinnamon; mix well
- Add apples, toss to coat
- Place apple mixture into an 8 or 9-inch baking dish
- Prepare topping in medium bowl
- Combine brown sugar, flour, rolled oats and cinnamon
- Cut in butter until the mixture is crumbly
- Stir in the walnuts
- Sprinkle topping evenly over the apples
- Bake at 350°F for 40 to 45 minutes or until apples are tender

Serves 6 to 8

Apricot Pudding

6 slices	Bread
2 cans	Apricot halves, drained and halved (reserve liquid)
½ cup	Butter
Pinch	Salt
1 tsp	Cinnamon
½ tsp	Nutmeg
6 Tbsp	Honey
3 Tbsp	Corn flakes

Preheat oven to 350°F

- Toast the bread and cut it into ½ inch cubes, set aside
- In a large sauce pan, mix ½ cup of apricot syrup with the butter, salt, nutmeg, cinnamon and honey
- Heat gently until well mixed
- Add the bread, apricots and corn flakes to the syrup mixture; toss together lightly
- Spoon mixture into a large greased ovenproof dish and bake at 350°F for 30 to 40 minutes
- Serve hot or cold with cream or ice cream

Serves 4

Bread Pudding

1 cup	Milk
½ cup	Cream
½ tsp	Vanilla
2	Eggs, beaten
3 Tbsp	Sugar
2 Tbsp	Butter, softened
8 slices	Bread, quartered
¼ cup	Raisins
	Rind of one lemon, grated

Preheat oven to 350°F

- Mix the milk, cream and vanilla in a saucepan; bring to a boil
- Remove from heat and let cool
- Beat the eggs and sugar together until pale and thick; then whisk in the milk
- Butter the bread and layer it in a greased pie pan with the raisins and lemon rind
- Pour the egg/milk mixture over the bread
- Bake at 350°F for 40 to 45 minutes or until pudding is set and golden on top

Serves 4

Wafer Dessert

Mixture #1

3	Egg whites
Pinch	salt
½ cup	Brown sugar
1 tsp	Vanilla

Mixture #2

20	Graham wafers, crushed
½ cup	Fine, unsweetened coconut
½ cup	Walnuts, chopped fine
½ cup	Sugar

Preheat oven to 325°F

- Beat the egg whites until foamy; add pinch of salt and continue beating until stiff
- Add ½ cup brown sugar and the vanilla; beat again until sugar is dissolved
- Combine mixture #2 ingredients together in a bowl
- Gently fold into the egg mixture
- Place batter in a cake pan and bake at 325°F for 45 to 50 minutes

Serves 6 to 8

Christmas Pudding

2 cups	Raisins
2½ cups	Currants
4 cups	Flour
1 cup	Brown sugar
1 tsp	Baking soda
½ tsp	Salt
½ tsp each	Cinnamon, nutmeg, allspice
4 cups	Butter
4 cups	Bread crumbs
1 cup	Mixed peel
½ cup	Molasses
1 cup	Milk
5	Eggs, beaten well

- Wash and dry raisins and currants, set aside
- Combine flour, sugar, baking soda, salt and spices with the butter and bread crumbs
- Add mixed peel then the raisins, currants, molasses, milk and beaten eggs, blend well
- Divide into three well-greased pudding bowls, cover with a buttered paper and then tie a cloth over it
- Place the bowl into a large pot of water and boil for 5 hours
- The water should come ¾ up the side of the bowl; keep topping it up as the water boils off
- When done, remove from saucepan and, take off the cloth; let cool then store in a dry place
- Before serving, boil again for 2 hours
- Serve with the following sauce:
    - In top of double boiler combine 1 cup syrup with ½ cup cream, heat through and keep warm
    - Just before serving beat in ½ cup melted butter and 2Tbsp brandy
    - Pour over pudding

Makes three small puddings

Preserves

Pickled Plums

3 pounds	Plums, not too ripe
1 Tbsp	Ginger root, finely chopped
1 tsp	Ground cloves
1 tsp	Ground cinnamon
2 Tbsp	Ground allspice
1 Tbsp	Salt
1½ cup	Sugar
2 cups	Vinegar

- Wash the plums and prick with a needle, set aside
- Put all other ingredients into a large sauce pan and cook slowly until boiling; stirring occasionally
- Add the plums and simmer gently for about five minutes
- Spoon the plums into sterilized jars
- Continue boiling the syrup until it thickens
- Pour syrup over the plums
- Seal and store for 2 months before eating

Makes about 4 pints

Apple and Blueberry Jam

1 pound	Apples, peeled, cored and sliced
1 cup	Water
1 pound	Blueberries
4 cups	Sugar

- Place the apples and water into a sauce pan; simmer gently until soft
- Add the blueberries; bring to a boil and simmer until blueberries are soft
- Stir in the sugar until dissolved
- Boil for about 10 minutes to setting point
- Stir well and pour into warmed jars

Makes about two 8-oz jars

Apple Chutney

3 pounds	Apples, finely chopped
1 pound	Onions, finely chopped
1½ cups	Sugar
½ cup	Water
2 Tbsp	Ginger root, finely chopped
1 tsp	Ground cinnamon
3	Red chillies, chopped
½ Tbsp	Salt
1½ cups	Vinegar

- Combine all ingredients and bring to a boil
- Simmer until mixture thickens
- Ladle into sterilized jars
- Seal right away and store 3 months before using

Makes about 5 pints

Fruit Mince

1½ pounds	Apples
3 pounds	Pears
3 pounds	Plums
1½ pounds	Raisins
1	Orange
1	Lemon
6½ cups	White sugar
1½ tsp	Ginger
1 Tbsp each	Cloves, cinnamon, nutmeg and allspice

- Quarter and core the apples and pears; remove the seeds
- Remove stones from the plums
- Cut orange and lemon into quarters, remove seeds
- Put all fruit into a food processor and chop
- Put sugar, ginger and spices into a large saucepan
- Add fruit mixture; bring to a boil and simmer for 40 minutes
- Pack into sterilized jars and process for 25 minutes

Makes about 9 pints

Edwards Brothers Malloy
Oxnard, CA USA
January 18, 2016